Beside
Every
Great
Dad

Beside Every Great Dad

Nancy L. Swihart
Ken R. Canfield

Tyndale House Publishers, Inc.
WHEATON, ILLINOIS

Library of Congress Cataloging-in-Publication Data

Canfield, Ken R.
    Beside every great dad / Ken R. Canfield, Nancy L. Swihart.
      p.   cm.
    Includes bibliographical references.
    ISBN 0-842333-1103-3 :
    1. Father and child. 2. Husbands—Family relationshps.
  3. Parenting—Religious aspects. I. Swihart, Nancy L. II. Title.
    HQ756.C357 1993

    306.874'2—dc20   92-43412

Printed in the United States of America

99 98 97 96 95 94 93
8   7   6   5   4   3   2

*For those who
have faithfully
stood beside us:*

*JUDD, DEE,
AND JEAN*

Acknowledgments

1 Fathers Who Love Their Wives *1*
by Ken R. Canfield

2 Mothers Who Love Their Husbands *11*
by Nancy L. Swihart

Part One
Understanding Your Child's Father
by KEN R. CANFIELD

3 Seek First to Understand *21*

4 How Your Husband Feels about Being a Father *33*

5 What Your Husband *Does* as a Father *59*

6 Obstacles Your Husband Faces as a Father *83*

7 Ways a Wife Can Hinder a Father *101*

Part Two
Encouraging Your Child's Father
by NANCY L. SWIHART

8 Deal with Your Own Past *121*

9 Stand Tall in the Yoke *139*

10 Pray for Your Husband *155*

11 Provide a Shelter of Honor *171*

12 Provide a Shelter of Acceptance and Comfort *185*

13 Give Him Space *199*

14 Give Him Feedback 213

15 Forgive Him When Necessary *231*

Epilogue: The Driving Force *249*

Appendixes
Mothers in Special Situations
by THE NATIONAL CENTER FOR FATHERING

A: Fathers and Daughters *255*
B: Fathers as Spiritual Leaders *263*
C: Hope for Single Mothers *271*
D: Stepfathers *281*
E: Abusive Fathers *287*
Notes *297*

A c k n o w l e d g m e n t s

Quality books that are written in this era utilize a team of gifted people. This book is the result of such a team.

The authors gratefully acknowledge the staff of the National Center for Fathering and Tyndale House Publishers. Special recognition is given to Lowell Bliss, who did a masterful job of reshaping and engineering the manuscript to its present form. Brock Griffin contributed to the flow and technical aspects of the writing and helped draft the appendixes. Both Lowell and Brock worked through the final punchlist to ensure quality and check for accuracy.

At Tyndale House, LaVonne Neff and Diane Eble gave valuable suggestions and provided ongoing feedback that helped to clarify the direction of the book.

Several readers have contributed their remarks: Kay Bascom, Kathy Bascom, Stephanie Moser, and Margaret Burton.

To all the above, we sincerely appreciate your contributions.

1 Fathers Who Love Their Wives

by KEN R. CANFIELD

Being an effective father to his kids is one of the most important tasks a man will face during his lifetime. I strongly believe this, and I know you agree, because you probably feel the same way about being a mother. The call to effective parenting is a high one indeed.

The marvelous thing about good fathering is that it will also provide your husband with some of the greatest rewards he will experience as a man. Often those rewards are subtle: the soft squeeze of a child's hand that communicates to a father he is loved, or perhaps some small incident that gives him a vision of the heritage he is passing on to his sons and daughters, and *their* sons and daughters.

But there will come a time for a more substantial reward. I can only speculate what will happen. As we stand before a glorified multitude, our Savior's speech may go something like this: "Well done, good and faithful servants. People are called to many different tasks; I called you men to be husbands and fathers, and I entrusted you with wives and children—to me, some of the most precious people in the world—and you did a wonderful job. Thank you."

I pray (along with the rest of the staff here at the National Center for Fathering) that your husband will be among that number of strong, faithful fathers. As he steps forward he'll notice something. He'll see that he was never alone in this task; there were others who helped him father his kids. And he'll take the hand of the one *beside* him, as together he and you step toward the throne.

In that moment, the protest won't even enter his mind: "Hey, wait a minute. He said *fathers.* That's me; the reward's mine alone." Instead, he will fully understand that while men—himself included—must take full responsibility for their fathering, they can never presume to take full credit when they've done well. Effective fathers very seldom walk alone.

In my case, I know the person beside me very well indeed. She is my wife, Dee, a woman worthy of double honor for all she has done to help me be a better father to my children.

Beside every great dad is a great wife. God bless you, Dee. God bless you, wives and mothers. Speaking on behalf of your husbands, God bless you.

Heroically Carrying the Load

God bless you for what you *do* for us fathers, but also for what you've *done:* You've carried the ball in our nation's families, the ball that so many of us men have dropped.

I'd love to gather your great-grandmother, your grandmother, your mother, and you, all in one room. To me, it would be an assembly of heroines, and I would listen intently to what you four had to say about how fathering and families have changed through the generations. Since the Industrial Revolution, most fathers have been pulled out of the home. The factory whistles blew, and the pressures and challenges of work prevented them from connecting positively with their children. (Maybe your dad or your husband is among this number.)

But our children were not left like orphans, because you mothers stepped in to fill the gap, nurturing our kids, teaching them, protecting them, listening to them, even providing for them. Sometimes mothers have had to do it *all*. It's a big task, to be both mother and father. Too big, in fact.

At least your work is not going completely unnoticed. I am confident that God is pleased. A whole generation of children is rising up and calling you blessed. And there are even some men who are noticing! Following a speech I gave in Boulder, Colorado, I was standing around talking to a group of men. I noticed one fellow standing at the edge of the circle, patiently waiting his turn. When he finally stepped forward, the only thing he said was this: "My wife has been the one to stand in the gap, and the success of our children is largely a credit to her." This man had a longing in his heart simply to honor his wife. I hope he went home and said to her what he told me that day.

What Fathers Say about Their Wives

I am the executive director of the National Center for Fathering. For five years we have been researching what makes a dad successful, what he can do to become engaged in the lives of his children in positive ways. Over these years, the Center has accumulated what we believe is the world's largest data bank on fathering. We have collected data on the practices and attitudes of over five thousand North American fathers. The things they say can be fascinating, inspiring, alarming, humbling, and heartbreaking.

It is our mission to help men like your husband become better dads. Naturally, we're very interested in identifying the resources that have been the most helpful to them. At one point we decided to come right out and ask, "Who has most influenced you in your fathering?"

Some men said, "my own father"; others said, "my pastor"; and a few even said, "James Dobson." But one of the most popular answers was, "my wife." As a wife, you have a vital influence on your husband's fathering, probably more than you realize. Let me repeat: While men must take the full responsibility for their fathering, they cannot take the full credit when they've done well. Beside every great dad is a great wife.

We asked each father to describe his wife's influence on his relationship to his kids. One man wrote, "Excellent," and underlined it, with two exclamation points at the end. "Understanding and loving and caring," wrote another man. As is often the case with men, the answers were short: "supportive" was the most common response. But what a response, and what a tribute to wives! The vast majority of men in our sampling appreciated their wives for being supportive influences on their fathering.

I recently published a book entitled *The 7 Secrets of Effective Fathers*. In the research for the book, we at the National Center for Fathering identified seven areas where effective fathers differed in their fathering from all other dads. One of the secrets that emerged was that an effective father is committed to a loving relationship with the mother of his children. The father loves his wife, and that stability enables him to be a better dad. You probably didn't need any research to tell you that, but what it told me was that fathers apparently hold a different perspective on parenting than mothers do. When your husband sets about to interact with his kids, he may not always view it as a one-on-one, father-child situation. You, as his wife, are not only in the picture; you are a primary influence. When he brings you in as part of his "fathering team," he gains insight and confidence. He becomes a more effective dad.

Fathers Need Their Wives

I am convinced I would not be as good a father if Dee were not such a supportive wife. I was the firstborn child in my family, but a great deal of my adventuresome spirit was stifled by my father, who, for all his virtues, ruled our household with strict discipline. I remember one day when Dee and I were living in Vancouver, British Columbia. She was pregnant with Joel, our third child, and we were walking along the hills by the shore with our two daughters, Hannah and Sarah. I was pulling the two little girls along in their red wagon, bouncing up on my toes, swinging my free arm out to my side, pulling in huge amounts of the fresh summer air with each breath.

As we came to the crest of a long hill, exuberance filled me. I hopped into the wagon behind Hannah and Sarah, grabbed the black steel handle, and with several powerful kicks sent us careening down the sidewalk. What adventure! I whooped and laughed, the girls cheered me on, and we must have reached speeds up to twenty mph before the terrain leveled out and we coasted to a halt.

It took a while for my pregnant wife to join the rest of us at the bottom, and as she plodded down to where we were waiting, I knew something was wrong. Dee "reflected back" to me just how dangerous our wild wagon ride might have been. But, God bless her, she spoke her mind in love, and we talked it through calmly. Dee helped me put my fathering into perspective and think more about my actions with my kids. But she also opened my eyes to an even greater lesson: For the first time in my fathering, I was able to see the connection between my past (how I was fathered) and my present (how I father). I wanted to be a free-spirited, exciting dad because my father had not been. Dee was not afraid to lovingly tell me how she felt, and as a result I became a better father.

I have not endured childbirth, but I've had five close encounters with it. I have participated in each of the deliveries, but there comes a point in the process where I cannot do a thing. The birth process is left up to Dee. I have come to believe that by virtue of carrying and bearing these children, she can see things in them and about them that I tend to miss completely. I desperately need to listen to her insight and understanding. The pain that women have to endure in childbearing and the intensity of this experience make me believe they are much more tuned in to their children; they can feel things that fathers cannot.

Women, your husbands need you.

An Invitation to Join the Team

The purpose of this book is to invite (and equip) you to join your husband's fathering team. We at the National Center for Fathering are convinced that, for the health of families in society, this book needed to be written. Men across the country are awakening to the joys and responsibilities of being a family man. I recently returned from a conference in Colorado where twenty-three thousand men gathered to declare their intention to be better husbands, fathers, and sons of God. How can they accomplish this? Only if their wives affirm those commitments and join their husbands as encouraging partners.

We asked Nancy Swihart to coauthor this book. You will hear her voice in the next chapter and in Part 2. Her husband, Judd, is one of the most effective fathers I know, mainly because Nancy is one of the best wives I know. She has struggled, as you will read, but she has also persevered by doing what she knows to do, and leaving the rest to the grace of God. Judd and Nancy have three kids. She has worked both in and out of the home, and presently is an English instructor at a local Christian college. Throughout this book, her experiences and insights will be combined with the latest research from the National Center for Fathering.

Not Just "One More Thing to Do"

On behalf of your husbands I invite you: Please join us. We need you. You may be saying, "But *my* husband doesn't even *want* to be encouraged as a father. He's skipped out of that role." Nancy and I will address such situations—how to encourage your husband even when he doesn't want to be a better dad. There is certainly a point where your responsibility ends, and we'll offer suggestions for knowing how to discern that point and what to do.

And yet, when we say that you will be a crucial and respected member of your husband's fathering team, we still mean it. Your husband needs your encouragement, even if he doesn't want it. And you *will* be respected for your encouragement, if not by your husband, then by me and, I believe, by God.

You may feel like Nancy and I are piling yet one more task on top of all you already have to do as a wife, mother, and woman. I am reminded of a brief description that Elisabeth Elliot once gave of the women of the stone-age Auca tribe in Ecuador: "Women wove hammocks and made pots and caught fish with their hands, cleared underbrush, planted crops, and carried by far the heaviest loads, while men chopped down trees and hunted, caught fish with nets and spears, and carried no loads at all if there was a woman around."[1]

But civilization has changed all that, hasn't it?

Hardly. Nancy and I know that you probably have been or are a young mother with kids at home. Your family income makes for a tight budget, and you may be working part-time or possibly even full-time. Your family is one of your main concerns, so you keep racing back and forth trying to meet their needs. In fact, it could be that the only reason you have found time to read this chapter now is because your daughter is at gymnastics and your son is at band practice. I won't even mention other demands, like church committees.

The Benefits of an Encouraged Dad

Being an encourager to your husband is a servant's role, and in a way it *is* "one more thing to do," but it comes with three very wonderful promises.

First, your children will benefit tremendously from having a more involved, more confident dad in their lives. *Fathers are important.* Studies of children who grew up without fathers in the home show that they are at risk: They're more likely to drop out of high school, more likely to score lower academically, more likely to engage in drug and alcohol abuse, and more likely to engage in delinquent behavior. [2] Anything you can do to encourage your husband to engage in his children's lives will benefit them immensely.

Second, an active father will lighten your own load as a parent. The more he parents, the less you'll have to. Our research underscores common sense: Fathers who feel satisfied with the support they receive from their wives are much more likely to praise and encourage their children than those who are unsatisfied with their wives' support. So as you encourage your husband and give him positive feedback, he grows more confident. The more confident he grows, the more likely it will be that he'll pull his own weight—and, who knows, maybe some of yours—in your parenting team.

Third, if you come from a background where your own father was not all you wanted him to be, investing yourself in your husband's fathering of your children can be a healing experience.

My friend Sally came from an abusive background—her father punished her severely and criticized her daily. Her biggest difficulty in life is trying to learn that not all men are like her father. Sally now has three beautiful daughters who have become the joy of her life. When she first saw her husband playing with her daughters and interacting with them on an emotional level, she would begin to quietly cry, though she had no idea why the tears came.

Then one day she realized that her husband was the kind of father she wished she'd had. Her husband was modeling before her the physical and emotional nurturance that every father can and should demonstrate. By encouraging her husband to express his fathering, she is allowing her feelings about fathers in general (based on her own abusive father) to change for the better. She is receiving healing for herself and the hope of a better life for her children.

There Are No Guarantees, But There Is a God

Despite these promises, there is one promise that Nancy and I cannot make, namely, that your husband will change. It's likely he will. My study of men has shown me that an encouraging wife is a powerful catalyst. But in the end, there is no guarantee that your husband will be different, even if you've mastered every principle we suggest. In fact, it's dangerous to begin this book with the goal of changing your husband. I don't need research to know this fact; I can recognize it inside myself as a man. If we men perceive that our wives are trying to change us, then we'll view even their best intentions as manipulative scheming. Forgive our pigheaded-ness, but it's really human nature. Wives often feel the same way.

But it's as much for *your* own sake that you should not try to change your husband. It will introduce a dynamic that will poison your relationship and undermine your best intentions.

Instead of trying to change him, simply do what you believe God has called you to do in relation to him and his fathering. Your faithfulness is within your control—the results are not. Above all else, place your faith in the one who has declared himself "a father to the fatherless, a defender of widows" (Psalm 68:5, NIV), the one who is on record as saying he will "turn the hearts of the fathers to their children" (Malachi 4:6, NIV).

Your best model may be the persistent widow whose story is told in Luke 18. When this woman pleaded for jus-tice, it very well could have been on behalf of her fatherless children. The lesson of that parable is not that God is a ruth-less judge, stingy with his blessings. Instead, the parable is a contrast. If a mother's persistence can finally win an evil judge's justice, how much more quickly will a loving heav-enly Father respond to the prayers of his widows and orphans.

Please, stick with it. Most of us men are reluctant to admit it, but we really do need you.

2 Mothers Who Love Their Husbands

by NANCY L. SWIHART

A few years ago my husband, Judd, and I acquired a rather large and dusty but very powerful symbol of what we want to accomplish in our marriage. The massive old oxen yoke that hangs in our barn is a token of other times, times when perhaps our world was more closely connected to living and natural symbols of interdependence. When the oxen were hitched to that yoke they automatically became a team. Their success in pulling their burden depended directly on how well they pulled together. When one ox was a little lame or tired, the other had to pull harder. When one would pull out in front or lag behind, the burden became too heavy for either to bear. Yokes demanded that the two burden bearers work carefully alongside each other.

By God's design, we are yoked together with our husbands in marriage. Usually it is a warm and comforting thought to know that we are not alone in this task of parenting. The quality of our teamwork will be reflected, not only in the marriage relationship, but also in the nurturing of our children.

On one side of the yoke, we bring our own strengths and weaknesses. On the other side, our husbands bring their world, with its own pressures and advantages. At times we feel the extra surge of strength coming from their side of the yoke; at other times we are reminded that we are affected by their weaknesses as we feel the yoke tighten and pull on our

own shoulders, and we are forced to support the lagging
end of our husband's side.

The Most Important Man in the World

If this book does nothing else, I hope it will *inspire* you as a
wife to invest yourself in your husband's fathering, to encourage him to become an effective and successful dad. I, like
you, have grown tired of the barrage of media messages that
try to convince me that perhaps fathers aren't important,
that maybe they are meant to be kept at the periphery of parenting, where they can cause as little damage as possible.
I've seen Dagwood Bumstead bumbling across the comic
pages. I've heard Dan Quayle get blasted for questioning the
wisdom of an unwed Murphy Brown. I've sat in college classrooms and heard the Freudian theories saying that, really,
only mothers matter.

But then I've also sat in our living room and watched my
husband playing with our children, Derrick, Dan, and Sara.
During those times it was perfectly clear: Their father is
important. I saw plainly that I don't have it in me to be everything my children need. Even if I were some kind of Super-
woman (and I am not), I would still only be able to supply
them with the wealth of the feminine, wondrous though it is.
It takes a man—preferably their father—to provide the deep
masculine input that rounds out their world and opens up
the mysteries of adulthood. Children need their fathers.

Of course, more and more research is confirming the
importance of an involved father in the home. In the previous chapter, Ken Canfield quoted one study that showed
the increased risks faced by fatherless children: drug and
alcohol abuse, poor school performance, etc. Another fascinating study occurred in Israel. A hospital observed the
development of fifty premature babies from birth until they

were eighteen months of age. Preterm infants whose fathers
visited them regularly in the hospital developed more
quickly and were able to leave the hospital sooner than
those whose fathers rarely stopped by.[1] What was happening? Spirit calling to spirit? DNA recognizing DNA?

Whatever we conclude from this and other studies, the
fact is that your husband is the most important man in the
world to your children. How he fathers will determine much
about how they grow up—and that can be a frightening
thought. Sometimes it's scary to acknowledge that so much
is outside our motherly control.

In God's grace, though, we are not responsible for how
our husbands father, in the same way that we are not ultimately responsible for how our children turn out. Our husband and our children are their own persons, who will make
their own decisions before God. Our responsibility is to be
faithful to what God has called us to do as wives and
mothers, to do what we can and leave the results to God.

All That a Wife Can Do

That's the other inspiring thing: There's a lot we *can* do to
help our husbands become better fathers. Ken and the
National Center for Fathering would not have asked me to
help write this book if many men just like your husband
hadn't said, "Our wives are the most powerful influences in
the way we father."

One study in the *Journal of Clinical Child Psychology*
reported that a father's lack of fathering skills is often linked
to increased marital conflict.[2] In other words, a father's ability to be an effective father corresponds closely with his marital relationship, his teamwork with his wife. Children need
their fathers, and fathers need their wives.

It's nice to feel needed.

Of course, there is another way to look at this. We wives may be the most powerful influence on our husbands' fathering, but that does not necessarily mean we are always a *positive* influence. We also have a remarkable ability to hinder their efforts at fathering. In the previous chapter, when Ken listed answers from the survey question, "Describe your wife's influence on your relationship to your kids," he spared us some of the more troubling answers. While the vast majority of men gave positive responses, we must also acknowledge the others. One man said his wife's influence was "counterproductive"; another called it "damaging." One man wrote: "When she puts me down in front of the kids, whether it's for being lazy or because we disagree on discipline or we have arguments, the kids get the message that it's okay to not listen to Dad because Mom is in control."

What does this do to our yokemate imagery? Are these oxen hitched to the same yoke but facing different directions? Does such a team of oxen just stand there, unable to move at all? Or perhaps they rotate around and around in a circle, not really going anywhere. Of course the children who depend on this team don't go anywhere either.

For better or worse, the yoke is in place, and now we have a choice to make. I say, let's use our influence for the benefit of our children, our husbands, and ourselves, in cooperation with God's plan for our families. Let's encourage our husbands to be better dads.

A Plan of Action

My second desire for this book is that it would actually *equip* you to encourage your husband effectively in his fathering.

With that in mind, we've divided the book into three parts. The first part involves understanding your husband as a father. Ken wrote this section, taking a look at "what husbands wish their wives knew about men as fathers" (to play off a James Dobson title). The first step in encouraging your husband is understanding him, which can be a difficult task. I hear complaints from many a wife whose husband is tight-lipped about what's brewing inside him. Our concerns may be perfectly valid, but we also need to realize that when men act as parents, they are not simply male mothers; they are *fathers*. We need to understand this unique perspective without projecting our own thoughts and emotions on their role. How does your husband view the task of fathering? What fears might he possess? What are some of the unique pressures he faces in the 1990s which work against effective fathering?

Understanding our husbands as fathers is the first step toward becoming effective encouragers, as we begin to learn where they need our help. Just as importantly, a sincere attempt to understand will keep us from the attitude that we are out to change them. Instead, we should accept the fact that change is something they may or may not do. Our responsibility is to love, understand, and encourage.

I have contributed the second part of this book, which deals with very practical ways we can help our husbands. Ironically, some of these activities focus on ourselves, not on our husbands. For example, one of the first suggestions is to deal with our own past, more specifically our feelings toward and relationship with our own fathers. The other practical steps are: become women of strength, pray strategically for our husbands, provide a shelter, give them space, provide feedback, and forgive them when necessary.

The appendixes (written by the staff at the National Center in collaboration with Ken) will address special situations such as encouraging fathers of daughters, encouraging our husbands to be spiritual leaders in our homes, dealing with divorce and the fathering void that results, encouraging step-fathers, and dealing with a husband who is an abusive father.

A Special Note to Special Wives

A special note here to those of you whose husbands are hard to encourage: Ken and I don't want to be naive. It's likely that some of you reading this book are married to men who are substantially dysfunctional, maybe even abusive, in their fathering. Such a situation can easily push a wife into her own very unhealthy patterns, one of which is adopting the role of an enabler. Rather than confront the problem directly—which is always painful—it's easy to fall into the trap of covering up for behavior, as my friend Jim's mother did. He told me, "My dad was a workaholic, but my mom was an enabler of his behavior. Whenever we asked why he was so busy or why he seemed so distant even when he was home, she'd always say, 'Oh, but of course your dad loves you. Can't you see how hard he works to provide for you?'"

If you struggle with a dysfunctional husband, we have a word of hope for you. Approaching your husband's fathering from the role of an encourager, not an enabler, can provide you with a great deal of freedom as you move toward your own personal healing. We'll try to be sensitive to the difficult situations, and we'll attempt to help you define the boundaries: what you can do to improve the situation, when you have fulfilled your responsibilities, and when you need to leave the matter in the hands of God.

For those of you who are single mothers, whose husbands, for whatever reason, are not in the home where they can be active fathers: It's true that your task is more difficult, but we believe that the principles and practical suggestions still apply in most cases. Your children still need a father. And this father figure, whoever he may be, still needs to be encouraged.

For divorced mothers, often the child's father is still around, though perhaps not very involved. These fathers need a great deal of encouragement. One study showed that within two years following a divorce, the average father will have little or no contact with his children.[3] Perhaps he gets pushed away by a bitter wife or a stringent legal system. Perhaps he loses his sense of priority. Often he just loses heart. Whatever the case, your children suffer as a result.

But even if the children's father is nowhere to be seen or is deceased, you as a mother can do a great deal to foster the "fathering component" for your children. This book can awaken you to the need to recruit and encourage healthy male role models (perhaps Grandpa, an uncle, a teacher, or a coach) who can fill the gap for your fatherless children.

Part One

Understanding Your Child's Father

by KEN R. CANFIELD

3 Seek First to Understand

When my wife, Dee, was pregnant for the first time, I remember noticing peculiar changes in her daily habits. She faithfully quit drinking coffee, took vitamins, and began going to bed much earlier. As the baby inside her grew, afternoon naps became a regular part of her schedule. A few months before the birth I found myself assembling baby furniture and helping her redecorate the bedroom, including a new shade of paint and new carpet. Then we waited. And waited.

Through the entire process, she clearly enjoyed her first experiences of motherhood—the planning, preparing, and bonding with the child inside her. Sometimes I'd catch her staring out the window, focusing on nothing in particular, probably thinking about the "coming day." She didn't even notice me watching her. When I asked what she was thinking or feeling, she'd look at me as if she had just been awakened from a dream that was too good to be true. "It's hard to explain," she'd say, turning back to the window. How could she put the meaning of motherhood into words?

But after Hannah was born I sensed that the roles had reversed somehow; now Dee was watching me stare at our newborn child. I would carefully count her toes and fingers, sometimes twice a day. I was completely in awe, and my amazement seemed to grow as we brought each of our five children home from the hospital.

I noticed that there was something different about the way I held our children, and I think it made Dee uncomfortable at first. She liked to cuddle them close to her body, while I held them out on my forearms, cradling their head in my palms and staring into their eyes. Or sometimes I would carry them around the house like a sack of potatoes.

At such times I think Dee began to sense that I wasn't having her motherly experience with our child; I was having a *father's* experience. What I experience as a parent is different from what she experiences as a parent, even though we are both parents, and parents of the same children.

No doubt you, too, have noticed a difference in how your husband relates to your children. Of course, sometimes these musings about differences aren't just quiet moments of wonderment; they can be alarming. Like when your husband suddenly throws your baby up in the air, and you're hoping he'll remember to catch her on the way down. Or when, in the middle of an emotional family crisis, your husband thinks nothing about heading off to work, able to focus on his daily duties until he arrives home later that evening, ready to pick up where he left off. How can we men do that? Why do we do that?

What goes on inside a man's head?

The first step in helping your husband become a better father is to attempt to understand what it means to him to be a father.

First Things First

Your tendency may be to want to rush on: "Just tell me what I need to do to whip this man into shape." You may feel the temptation to jump to the second section of this book, where Nancy does give practical suggestions on ways to encourage your husband. But if you miss taking time to simply under-

stand who your husband is, then you've missed everything.
You've guaranteed that those practical suggestions of Part 2
won't work.

Stephen Covey has a chapter in his book *The Seven Habits of Highly Effective People* entitled "Seek First to Understand, Then to Be Understood." His thoughts below could
be the thoughts of your husband:

> Unless I open up with you, unless you understand me
> and my unique situation and feelings, you won't know
> how to advise or counsel me. What you say is good and
> fine, but it doesn't quite pertain to me.
>
> You may say you care about and appreciate me. I des-
> perately want to believe that. But how can you appreci-
> ate me when you don't even understand me? All I have
> are your words, and I can't trust words.
>
> . . . Unless you're influenced by my uniqueness, I'm
> not going to be influenced by your advice.[1]

We urge you to begin by seeking to understand your husband—how he views and goes about his fathering—for
three important reasons: it can *inform* how and where you
need to encourage him; it can *motivate* you to encourage
him; and it can *express* the unconditional love which makes
encouragement acceptable. Let's look at each of these a little
closer.

Where to Apply the Salve

Understanding your husband is important because it
informs the way you encourage him. The word *encouragement* itself means to "infuse with courage." How will you

know where courage is needed unless you identify the particular fears that your husband associates with fathering?

A woman I know grew more and more frustrated because
her husband wasn't spending enough time with their two
daughters. Her concern was genuine—she watched how fast
her kids were growing, and she knew her husband was miss-
ing out. One day he'd look back, sorry that his kids' early
childhood had gone by largely without him. *What he needs,*
she told herself, *is some discipline in choosing his priorities.*
She decided that if she gave her husband a chunk of
unstructured time with the children, he would get a little
more used to putting them first. So this wife arranged an out-
ing for herself. She went to visit a friend for the evening, leaving the husband with no choice but to stay home with the kids.

When she came home, the first one to meet her at the
door was her two-year-old, whose diaper had not been
changed for several hours and whose bottom was beet red
with a rash. The baby in the crib was crying uncontrollably.
Her husband came running out of the bedroom with a
shaken, frantic look in his eyes. At that moment, he was
probably less devoted to his fathering than ever. This wife's
well-reasoned plan had backfired. She thought he needed
one thing (disciplined priorities), when really he needed
another (some simple ideas to strengthen his parenting).
Because she didn't know her husband, he was set up for failure, and the kids suffered.

The Sweet Intimacy of the Yoke

The second reason for taking the time to understand your
husband is that it heightens your motivation to serve him.
When Jesus uses the imagery of the yoke to signify the
work we do with him, he claims that his yoke is easy and his

burden is light (Matthew 11:30). Jesus' yoke is easy partly
because so much of the strength needed to pull the load is
coming from his side, not yours. But another reason you can
delight in the yoke and consider it a thing of ease is because
of the *connectedness* that it represents. There's a joy in walking so close to Jesus, matching him stride for stride, knowing him intimately.

In the same way, you are yoked with your husband in the
task of parenting; you know him and he knows you. Out of the
corner of your eye, you see his muscles strain against the
weight of an unruly kid. You revel in his lively gait as he trots
through a daughter's first Christmas. You hear his steady,
rhythmic breathing as he endures a son's drug addiction.

The times may be good or bad, but you are connected
with the man you've chosen to love for the rest of your life.
Seeking to understand him as a father can give you the first
whiff of a special intimacy, which is one of the choicest
rewards of joining with your husband in helping him father
your kids.

Giving Psychological Air

Finally, and most important, seeking to know your husband
conveys love and concern that is unconditional. Without
such unconditional love (the desire to love and understand
him regardless of what he becomes as a dad), your husband
will miss the environment where he can grow as a father.
Stephen Covey calls this environment "psychological air":

> If all the air were suddenly sucked out of the room
> you're in right now, what would happen to your interest
> in this book? You wouldn't care about the book; you
> wouldn't care about anything except getting air. . . .

When you listen with empathy to another person, you
give that person psychological air. And after that vital
need is met, you can then focus on influencing or problem solving. This need for psychological air impacts
communication in every area of life.[2]

You may long for your husband to be a better dad for any
number of reasons. Maybe you desire that he experience all
the joys and rewards that fatherhood offers, or that your children reap all the wonderful benefits of having an involved
father. Maybe you hope your own load as a parent will be
lightened when your husband starts "chipping in" a little
more. Maybe you're worried about your family's reputation
in the community, something that can be greatly enhanced if
your husband acts a little more like Bill Cosby and a lot less
like Homer Simpson. There may even be a secret joy in
being better than him at something (parenting), where
you're playing the role of expert and he's your pupil.

Your motivations may be mixed, and it's often difficult to
keep them pure, so you may want to take on this aspect of
marriage—seeking to first understand your husband as a
father—as a spiritual discipline. When you truly attempt to
empathize with someone, you force yourself to put your
thoughts of what that person ought to be, or what he'll be
when you're done with him, on hold. You simply want to know
who he is now, *as he is.* You accept him. When you do finally
get around to doing the practical activities that encourage and
influence him in his fathering, you have trained yourself to be
motivated by an interest *in his well-being,* because you have
first nurtured an interest simply *in his being.*

If the act of encouraging your husband is like the sowing
of good seed, then understanding him is like tilling and culti-

vating the soil beforehand. Seeking to deeply know your husband communicates that he is important to you whether he ever becomes an effective father or not. Such concern provides an atmosphere of acceptance and security, which makes it more likely that he *will* become an effective dad.

Letting Your Man Be a Man

Knowing your husband begins with being aware of a cultural dynamic at play with your husband. In colonial times, the care and nurture of children was seen as a father's central mission, a crucial part of his duty as a man. In 1774, before he became president, John Quincy Adams wrote these words to his wife: "Above all cares of this life, let our ardent anxiety be to mould the minds and manners of our children. . . . Pray remember me to my dear little babes, who I long to see running to meet me and climb upon me under the smiles of their mother. The education of our children is never out of my mind."[3]

Such sentiment from a man today might well get him labeled a wimp. This century's male exodus from the home has meant that parenting, by necessity, has become something that females do. (Just recently I read an article in *USA Today* claiming that in Detroit and Washington, D.C., mother-only families make up a majority of all families with children.[4]) Our culture has unfortunately made the leap to say that if parenting is something done primarily by females, then parenting must be a feminine pursuit.

Another recent *USA Today* headline read: "Men seeking more family time fear 'wimp factor.'" The issue in the article was paternity leave. A 1990 survey of two hundred *Fortune 1000* companies found that 30 percent of the companies had unpaid paternity leave policies, but only one percent of eligible men used them. Economics was an issue, but so appar-

Supporting Your Husband's Decisions in Front of the Children

Over 2,000 fathers were asked to rate their wives' support of their decisions on a scale ranging from poor to excellent. Their responses can be broken down as follows:

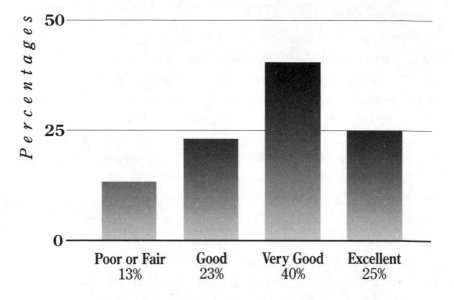

| Poor or Fair | Good | Very Good | Excellent |
| 13% | 23% | 40% | 25% |

How does a wife's support affect her husband's satisfaction as a father? Fathers who reported the least support rated their satisfaction between mixed and somewhat satisfied, while fathers reporting the highest degree of support reported themselves as somewhat satisfied to very satisfied.

ently was the "wimp factor." Ellen Galinsky of the Families and Work Institute claimed that a man taking paternity leave is "not seen as a young lion. He's not seen as serious and committed [to what men are supposed be serious and committed about]."[5]

Men fear being feminized. But when you seek to understand your husband and the unique emotions, activities, and obstacles of fatherhood, then you calm that fear. You communicate to him the following: "There is a distinctive contribution that you as a man make to the parenting of our children. It grows out of your masculinity. I want to know and understand what those distinctives are, so that as I encourage you to be a better father, I won't be trying to turn you into some male version of a mother. Instead, I'll be affirming and encouraging what God has placed in you as a man."

When Jesus entered into this world for the sake of God the Father's children, he remained 100 percent God even as he became 100 percent human. When your husband enters into the world of nurturing his kids, he can be both 100 percent parent and 100 percent man. As you attempt to understand what it means for your husband to be a father, you communicate to him: "You have the freedom to be a great dad."

Men of Few Words

Jack Balswick once wrote a book for men entitled *Why I Can't Say I Love You.* He tells a story about "the old Vermonter, married forty years, who remarked, 'I love my wife so much, sometimes I can hardly keep from telling her so.'"[6]

Sometimes I laugh at that joke. But I include it here because . . . well, sometimes I want to cry about it. I've been talking about the importance of understanding your husband, of knowing what he thinks and feels about fathering. Admittedly, this can be difficult to do if your husband is tight-lipped about what goes on inside him.

When I work with fathers, I consider it one of my greatest goals to get them out of their heads and into their hearts. Most men have not been trained by their fathers or the culture to access their emotional side. And yet, I have found that men will talk with emotion about their kids. At such times, I see God at work fulfilling his prophecy of Malachi 4:6, NIV: He will "turn the *hearts* of the fathers to their children."

If you feel your husband has built his emotional walls so high that you can never scale them, don't despair. In the next chapter, I'll provide you with some questions that he may be willing to answer. But for now, let me leave you with this section of Francis of Assisi's prayer:

> *O Divine Master,*
> *Grant that I may not so much seek*
> *To be consoled as to console;*
> *To be understood as to understand;*
> *To be loved as to love.*

Questions for Personal Reflection

Think about these before discussion group.

1. Has your husband displayed any interest in becoming a good father?

2. On a scale from one to ten, with one being low and ten being high, how would you rate his commitment to fathering?

3. What are your husband's greatest obstacles in fathering?

Questions for Discussion

To discuss with a small group

1. Have you ever belittled or intimidated your husband in his fathering?

2. Why are men often "unprepared" for the parenting process?

3. What has been the most helpful thing you have done to understand your husband?

4. What advice would you give to a young mother with two children as she seeks to understand her husband?

4 How Your Husband Feels about Being a Father

Blake Ashdown is the president of a successful resort business in Michigan. He is also the father of five children. Whenever Blake talks about fathering, he invariably makes this comment: "No man on his deathbed is going to turn to those around him and say, 'You know, I wish I had made some more money during my lifetime.' He's not going to say, 'Boy, I wish I could've knocked a few strokes off my golf game.' If he says anything of regret, it'll probably be, 'I wish I had spent more time with my family.'"

It's unfortunate that so much of what wives want to know about a man's thoughts and feelings must come from inference. The cultural icon of masculinity is the stoic cowboy out on the lonely plains, a man of few words and limited emotion. He can't stay and talk; he's too busy riding off into the sunset.

So you let the dust settle and stare at his back as his horse canters off into the distance, but because you still want to know him, you do the next best thing: you *infer* what's going on inside him by analyzing what goes on around him. As a result, it's easy to arrive at the conclusion—contrary to what Blake says—that many men are intrinsically more interested in making money and lowering their golf handicap than they are in being effective as fathers. Look at how much energy he invests in his hobbies. Calculate all the hours spent at the factory or office. Look at how little time he spends with his kids.

I'm hard-pressed to explain it. One study claims that in the United States, fathers spend as little as thirty-seven seconds a day in meaningful interaction with their young children.[1] It's kind of hard not to infer that many men don't place a high priority on fathering.

I refuse to explain away the tragic mess of misplaced priorities, but I do want to open your eyes to the possibility that something deeper may be going on under the surface of the priorities that get expressed at any one moment. Like Blake, I want to teach you about the essential emotions at work in your husband—the things that may get mentioned only on deathbeds. It may be that your husband is not even aware of these feelings himself. I'm talking about the issues that get to the condition of his *heart*.

Why Don't Fathers Father?

I believe that being a father is one of the most important and rewarding tasks a man will face in his lifetime. I identify it in myself, and I see it played out across the generations. I am also coming to the conclusion that *all* men—your husband included—also share this sense that fathering is important. It's bred in the bones. It's part of the Creation mandate given by God to our greatest grandfather, Adam. When God told Adam, "Be fruitful and increase in number; fill the earth and subdue it" (Genesis 1:28, NIV), he was talking not only about simple procreation but about a process of passing on the best of himself to posterity.

If this is the case, then why don't more men act as if fathering is important? Why do we live in a country where 19 million children are growing up apart from their biological fathers?[2]

Maybe in your family, you've wondered why your husband has occasionally acted like Sue's husband, Stephen.

Sue was spending her days at home with their three-year-old daughter, Bethany. Stephen had extra hours added to his shift at work. He was putting in ten-hour days. Sue decided to encourage him by working up an anticipation in Bethany for her daddy's arrival. "Daddy's coming home!" she'd say to Bethany as the time approached for Stephen to arrive. Bethany would smile and repeat her mother's words: "Daddy's coming home!" When Stephen finally did walk through the front door, Bethany stood just outside the circle of the door's swing. "Daddy's home! Daddy, you're home!" she shouted gleefully, bouncing up and down on her little feet.

Stephen walked on into the house—right past Bethany. He never noticed his devastated daughter trailing behind him. This went on for a week. Bethany became more and more puzzled, more and more crushed, more and more timid.

Why, if I believe that Stephen senses somewhere down inside himself that fathering Bethany is important, did he seem so impervious to her hunger for love as he walked on past? I've talked to Stephen; I know he believes fathering is important. Why does he—and maybe your husband—often act as if it's not important?

In this chapter, along with the joys accompanying fathering, we are also going to look at some of the deep-seated fears of fathering. Some men find these fears so paralyzing that they're unable to do what they know they need to do for their children. In the next chapter, we'll look at the responsibilities of fathering. Maybe one conclusion we'll be forced to reach is that some men are simply sinful and irresponsible; they refuse to do what they know they should do. In chapter 6 we'll look at the obstacles that the world places before men as they attempt to father.

There may be occasions in raising your children when you are tempted to think that your husband is your enemy,

standing in the way of all you desire for your children. I want
to convince you of this point: Your husband is not your
enemy. Satan is your enemy. Your husband's fears and sins
and obstacles concerning fathering are your enemy.

Those of us who love fathers—including wives like you
and fathering advocates like me—need to be careful not to
simply stop at the surface evidence. We need to plunge the
depths to truly understand what's going on in men's hearts.
Only then can we truly help and encourage them.

How does your husband view his fathering? When he
thinks about being a dad, how does he feel?

While all men are different, I would like to reveal to you
five negative emotions and five positive emotions which I
believe are at play in most men.

The Pains of Fatherhood

It would be wonderful to say that fatherhood is always an
intrinsically positive experience for men, that the joyful emotions are enough to keep your husband motivated throughout the toughest times. Unfortunately, being a dad also
entails some negative emotions.

Fathers feel these emotions most sorely during the tough
times of parenting. As a mother, you know that trials come.
Adolescence can be one of the most trying times. Our research at the National Center shows that a father's level of
satisfaction reaches its lowest level when his kids are in
their teens. The children are growing up and growing away.
They are pressing against boundaries and challenging their
parents. I have written in my book *The 7 Secrets of Effective
Fathers* of the man who is shaving one morning in the bathroom. He looks down and there is his son beside him, with
shaving cream also on his face, which he's scraping off with
his plastic toy razor. The man smiles: At such times, it's

good to be a dad. Twelve years later, he and his son are
again at that same mirror. But now the boy is leaning over
and pulling at his earlobe, trying to decide whether he
should get it pierced and what kind of earring to wear. It
may just be a phase, but it's a painful and complex one, and
it strains the relationship.

As a wife who loves her husband, you will want to monitor
the tough times of fatherhood and be aware of the five negative emotions often associated with fathering.

Anger

While it's true that men in our culture are expected to be
confident and under control, the one emotion that is cultur-
ally sanctioned for us is anger.[3] Men are "allowed" to be
angry; it's somehow macho. (Women, on the other hand, get
censured when they express anger.[4])

Anger is a complex emotion that, like any emotion, can
have a positive expression. But, also like any emotion, it
must be governed by self-control, which is a fruit of the Holy
Spirit. When it is not, anger can destroy. It is a precursor to
abuse, an issue of grave concern in parenting.

If your husband's anger leads to abuse, you need to take
steps to protect your children and yourself. You do not need
to read any further here and attempt to "understand" your
husband's anger or abuse. That can come later. Instead, turn
to appendix E. Right after that, please call a trusted friend
and confidante. Begin to take steps to remove yourself and
your children from the situation until your husband can get
help. I respect your desire to do all you can to help your husband be a better father. Making that phone call could well be
the first step. As a result, you will confront him with his
abuse and open his eyes to the harm he's brought his chil-

dren. By God's grace, he may respond to your courage by also seeking the professional help *he* needs.

Most of you, however, probably do not live in abusive situations. Nonetheless, it will help to understand the interesting connection between your husband's anger and his fathering.

One day, Bill got a call from his daughter at college. "Dad, could you wire me some money?"

"What's wrong, honey?" he asked. "Did something happen?"

"No, I just accidentally bounced a check. I haven't balanced my checkbook for a couple of months, and I lost track of how much was in my account. I'm only overdrawn by a few dollars."

Such things happen. But something was happening inside Bill, too. Something welled up inside him. He proceeded to give his daughter a lecture that ended with her hanging up on him and running to her dorm room in tears. He was fuming.

Bill's wife, Doris, watched all this, but when she finally got an explanation out of him, it still didn't make sense to her. What's a few dollars? Anyone can be careless with a checkbook now and then.

It didn't make sense because what was happening with Bill was psychological, not logical. Eventually, he called his daughter back to apologize and, out of his sense of guilt at his outburst, he wired more money into her account than necessary. Eventually, he also understood what happened.

Bill also has trouble handling money. He has bounced more than one check himself and eventually had to give the entire family financial duties over to his wife; he just wasn't able to manage it. His anger at his daughter in this incident was rooted in anger at himself. Throughout his life he's felt frustrated at not being able to overcome this particular weakness. Now he sees the same weakness in his offspring.

"A chip off the old block." "Like father, like son." "The acorns don't fall far from the tree." All these expressions tell us that our children inherit more than our money: They inherit our good traits and our bad ones too. Often when your husband gets angry at your child, it's not (totally) because of what the child has done. It can also be anger at himself as he sees his own weaknesses reflected back to him in his children.

You as his wife can help defuse this particular type of anger by taking care in how you use the phrase: "Our kids are just like you." Unknowingly, you may be taunting your husband, further highlighting in him those habits and vices he knows and hates and wishes he could overcome.

A Sense of Inadequacy

My friend Eric was one of the first men to verbalize to me a sense of inadequacy as a father: "Ken," he said, as we sat on the front porch and watched our kids playing across the street in the park, "I have *no* idea what I'm doing when it comes to this fathering stuff. I feel like a fish out of water."

All men have been trained in some part for their careers. Some have been trained extensively, with years in technical school, college, even graduate school. Even on the job, there are seminars to attend, manuals to study, supervisors to consult. Not so with fathering, one of the most important jobs your husband will ever have.

"Oh, I feel like I'm doing everything that's expected of me most of the time," Eric continued. "But even that's only by the grace of God, what with my job and everything. Usually, I feel like I'm just muddling through. I've got this fear that one day it's all going to crash down around me."

When your husband leaves the showroom with a new car,

there's an owner's manual waiting in the glove compart-
ment. When he drives home from the hospital with a new
baby, he's on his own.

A sense of inadequacy can paralyze a man. Here's this little life in your husband's arms: so precious, so fragile. In
fact, so precious and so fragile that he may be afraid to make
a move for fear of making the wrong move. Or, he's afraid to
make a move for fear of appearing foolish. Ronald Taffel is
the director of family and couples treatment at an institute in
New York. He comments: "Sometimes I think there is
greater fragility in the male ego around child-rearing than
there is even around sex. Men are so quick to establish a pattern of no confidence in their decisions—thus deferring
those decisions to women—that it makes feelings of sexual
inadequacy look like nothing."[5]

For a number of men, this sense of inadequacy translates
into a wonderfully teachable humility: "Honey," your husband might say to you, "being a good parent is important to
me. You are so good with the kids. Teach me what you
know." When such a man is matched with a wife who freely
invites him into the parenting team, the children reap the
benefit of two skilled caregivers.

For the man whose sense of inadequacy is paralyzing
him, understanding his fears and encouraging him are again
the best antidote. And there are still more ways to invite him
into the parenting team and build his confidence.

Embarrassment

In his book *Fatherhood,* Bill Cosby writes: "I must admit I
did ask God to give me a son because I wanted someone to
carry the family name. Well, God did just that, and I now con-

fess that there have been times when I've told my son not to reveal who he is.

"'You make up a name,' I've said. 'Just don't tell anybody who you are.'"[6]

We are well aware of those moments during adolescence when our compulsively self-conscious teenagers become embarrassed by their parents. "You can drop me off here, Mom," your daughter says.

"But we're still a block away from the mall."

"That's okay—I'll walk."

Fathers can feel the same way about being associated with their kids. Of course, for teenagers the embarrassment is usually just a phase, shallowly focused on the "old-fashionedness" and "geekiness" we adults supposedly represent. While a son's mohawk haircut or a daughter's media-copied clothing may also embarrass a father, more is usually at stake.

Remember, children bear their father's name. A man's name is at stake in the behavior and performance of his children. When the kids, for whatever reason, lose respect in society, the father feels it sorely.

Have you ever heard the expression, "Your name is mud"? In itself the phrase is descriptive: Your reputation is soiled and worth as much as dirt. Actually, the expression is even more revealing when you learn that the original phrase was: "Your name is *Mudd*." Mudd is the last name of Samuel Alexander Mudd, the physician who set John Wilkes Booth's leg after President Abraham Lincoln's assassination. A military court accused him of co-conspiracy.

All across the land, Mudd's reputation was despised. But not only his reputation—his name also, and all that bore that name. If Dr. Mudd's father was still alive at the time, no doubt he sorrowfully thought of his son, lamenting "the loss of all I've worked for." Proverbs 22:1 claims, "A good name is to be more desired than great riches." If this is one of the truths of the universe, then men feel it deep inside when their offspring do something to tarnish that name.

Unfortunately, fathers can overreact. Too often, when some children most need their parents' help (for instance, in the midst of drug abuse), some fathers distance themselves most fully. They may not go so far as to actually disown their children (though that's possible, through a legal process). But in less dramatic form, a father out of embarrassment can convey the message, "You're no child of mine." As with all five of these negative emotions, I'm not saying that a father *should* feel this way; I'm simply saying that he often *does* feel this way. We need to seek first to understand.

A Sense of Being Forgotten

Picture the following scenario: You are busy one evening, off to a meeting or out with friends. Your husband has the kids, and he's decided to take them down the street to the park. One of your children is sliding down the slide. Your husband pushes the other on the swings.

A female friend of yours walks into the park with two kids of her own. She recognizes your husband and walks over to where he is playing with the kids.

"Where's (your name)?" she asks.

"Oh, she's at a meeting tonight," your husband replies.

"Oh, so I guess you're _____ the kids tonight, huh?" she says.

Now, in your mind, how did you fill in the blank in the above comment? What do you think might normally be said there? Did your friend say, "Oh, so I guess you're *fathering* the kids tonight"? Did she say, "Oh, so I guess you're *per-*

forming one of the responsibilities God has given fathers by being actively involved with your children and seeing to their emotional and physical development"?

I doubt it.

More than likely, your husband was once again accused of simply *watching* or *baby-sitting* the kids in their mother's absence. "Oh, so I guess you're baby-sitting the kids tonight, huh?"

It's enough to make a man feel forgotten or left out of this parenting racket.

Anthropologist Margaret Meade is reported to have once said, "Men are a biological necessity, but a sociological absurdity," meaning that the only *fathering* that is necessary is the kind that occurs at conception. The debate whether Murphy Brown–type families (mother-only) are legitimate and viable alternatives hinged on the question of whether fathers are really important. Society can make fathers feel left out.

Admittedly, biology can also make a father feel on the side-lines. The first child-parent interactions occur during pregnancy and are largely reserved for the mother. The father is merely an observer. Remembering morning sickness, lower back pain, and labor, you might be inclined to say, "You haven't missed much, bub," but there are other special, tender moments. Take, for instance, breast-feeding. Your husband will never get to experience those natural, regularly occurring moments of parent nourishing child.

Many wives are also responsible for making their husbands feel left out. One question the National Center asked in its open-ended surveys was, "Has your wife ever discouraged you as a father?" One man's response was, "Yes—she wouldn't let me help with the kids in the earlier years, from birth to age three." Some wives bracket off the very early

years and post off-limits signs. My own mother and father
were this way. Other wives divide up the responsibilities so
that a father has a limited role throughout his fathering
career. Maybe you know a wife who expects her husband to
be involved with the children only in the areas of discipline
and helping with their homework, leaving all the nurturing
roles for herself to carry out.

A Sense of Being Alone

When Nancy Swihart was a young mother, she had the
invaluable privilege of a supportive network of friends. She
writes:

> When my children were little I lived for Tuesday morn-
> ings. The two boys, fifteen months apart, were very cre-
> ative in encouraging each other in all sorts of behavior
> that was exploratory and exciting for preschoolers, but
> exasperating for a young mother.
>
> However, after talking toddlerese all week, side-
> stepping toys every time I wanted to go through the liv-
> ing room, wiping runny noses a zillion times a day,
> Tuesday morning was "my" time. This was when a
> group of us young mothers would converge on the
> church, drop our children off at the nursery, and meet
> together to study and pray.
>
> At that stage of our lives, what we needed most was
> encouragement from each other. We needed to know
> others shared the struggles and triumphs of being at
> home with young children, whose demands required
> all the ingenuity we could muster just to get through
> each day. Here I was, a college graduate, finding more
> challenge in being a wife and mother than I had in my

toughest classes in college! We women recognized the urgent need for other adult input.

Such young mothers' groups are still prevalent across the country, though I suspect they are much harder to attend nowadays, when Tuesday mornings may find many mothers at the office. Nonetheless, I bet that you as a mother have a more extensive, more tightly woven, more emotionally integrated support network for your mothering than your husband does for his fathering. Your husband may not only feel alone; in fact he may be "going it alone."

Some men are awakening to their need to receive wisdom, accountability, and support from other men. This past summer, twenty-three thousand Christian men met in Boulder, Colorado. During the four days of meetings, I remember at least three different speakers who quoted Howard Hendricks' statement that "a man without a small group is an accident waiting to happen." Heads nodded in agreement across the stadium at these words, and throughout the weekend I saw groups of men huddled together, praying for each other. I saw older men with their arms around younger ones, sharing their wisdom.

The National Center has a 138-item questionnaire that men fill out concerning their fathering practice. They answer questions about how well they feel they are doing as a dad. A while back, I looked at the questionnaire and decided to test a hypothesis: I hypothesized that when men were confronted with answering over one hundred self-report questions specifically related to their fathering, they would in fact feel guilty and overwhelmed. So I devised a test. Early in the survey, I asked the men, "How do you feel about yourself as a father?" Over one hundred questions later in the same survey, I asked them the same question.

To my surprise, the men apparently began to feel better about their fathering as they got further through the survey. Their answers were more positive the second time the question was asked. This little exercise taught me that men actually take pleasure in being held accountable for their fathering. They want to be part of a larger group of supporters who will guide and encourage them as a dad.

As we've already stated at the beginning of this book, fathers especially want one person on their team: you, the wife. Your husband needs you. And he needs other men too—especially older men who have weathered the fathering storms before him and can chart the course.

Men want support. They are seeking it. But the vast majority are still modeling their lives on the cultural icon of the cowboy. Picture the Marlboro man, John Wayne, the Lone Ranger. The Lone Ranger never asked Tonto how to handle a strong-willed two-year-old. A very profound emotion among men—perhaps your husband included—is the sense of facing the task of fathering alone.

A man's sense of being alone often begins with feeling separated from his own father. If he was a fatherless child, he faces the task of fathering without the constant mental companion of his father's model. Even men who grew up with a father present in the home can miss out on support from their dads when it comes to being fathers themselves. Gordon Dalbey, author of *Fathers and Sons,* asks this question when he speaks to men: "How many of you men, when you had your first child, had a father who came up alongside you to teach you something about being a dad?" A few hands will be raised; Gordon estimates maybe three hands for every one hundred in the audience.

The sense of being alone is a curse that can be—and needs to be—broken. Fathering is neither a dreaded obligation nor a source of bondage, but a joy. And no matter how undernourished your husband feels due to his lack of positive fathering models, he *can* sense the same sort of accomplishment and fulfillment that you do as a mother. The help is out there, from you and from others, if your husband is willing to receive it.

The Joys of Fathering

The joys of fathering are rather slippery. It's not that they're uncommon or difficult to attain; in fact, there are many fathers who experience them every day. These joys are slippery because while fathers do have strong emotions, too few fathers understand and express those emotions, even if they feel extreme contentment or elation.

I had a baseball coach who told our team that it was good to lose a game or two early in the year because "people learn from failure." He may have been trying to make the best of our losses, but I believe there's some truth here. When a person succeeds at something, there's no reason to consider what he has done wrong and how he can improve the next time. But when he has failed, the immediate reaction is to want to figure out *why* it happened, and how it can be corrected.

When your husband experiences the joys of fathering, he probably doesn't stop to think about what has caused his satisfaction, or make a conscious effort to make it happen again. He is probably very well acquainted with the five emotions I'm about to describe, but he may not be able to put them into words. In an effort to help *you* understand and encourage him, I'm going to give it a try.

A Sense of Healing

We've talked a lot about fatherless children. We'd do well to recognize at this point that your husband may also be a fatherless child. Since 1950—likely the very time your husband was being born—the rate of divorce in America has doubled.[7] Many men grew up without a dad. Perhaps an even greater number grew up with an emotionally distant father. Some of you no doubt sense the wounds present in the man you married. You feel it when anger starts to simmer, and you occasionally catch a glimpse of the spiritual blood he bleeds.

Unfortunately, fatherhood can be the vehicle that transfers those wounds to the next generation. Research shows that a person who has been abused by his parents is very much at risk of being abusive to his or her own children as well.[8]

However, other men discover in fatherhood a means to break the cycle and find healing for themselves. For all men there's the expectant air of opportunity. They hold the newborn in their arms and think, "Things can be different between you and me." Whether or not they embrace that opportunity is another matter.

Many men jump at the chance for healing. Our research has shown that men who didn't have a committed father themselves make up one of the most vigorously committed groups of fathers. We call these "overcomer" fathers, or sometimes "compensatory fathers."[9] These fathers are eager to be the father they wish they'd had.

Once at a seminar we did in Seattle, a man came up to my colleague Judd Swihart (Nancy's husband) and said, "The more I hear about fathers, the more I want to become a kid." This man wasn't expressing some sort of irresponsible regression; he was simply recognizing the tendency fathering has to meld the generations. Effective fathers can in effect "re-father" themselves and experience healing as a result.

Here's how author H. W. Beecher expresses the experience:

> We never know the love of the parent till we become parents ourselves. When we first bend over the cradle of our own child, God throws back the temple door, and reveals to us the sacredness and mystery of a father's and a mother's love to ourselves. And in later years when they have gone from us, there is always a certain sorrow, that we cannot tell them we have found it out.[10]

Exodus 34:7 speaks of a four-generation curse of a father's sins upon his progeny, but Jeremiah writes of a new day, when "people will no longer say, 'The fathers have eaten sour grapes, and the children's teeth are set on edge'" (31:29-30, NIV; see also Ezekiel 18:1-4). God will break the inherited cycles of sin and pain.

When a man effectively fathers, he becomes aware of moments when he breaks a pattern that he knows has been destructive. At such times, he purposely and resolutely cuts off extended sin. It's a brave moment, designed to thrill a man's heart.

When it comes to joyful healing, first experiences—especially around the first child—seem to have the most impact. My father wasn't allowed to be there when I was born, and I've been told that he didn't really become involved in many aspects of my life until I was two or three years old. But when Hannah was first born, I was in a constant state of

amazement at what God had entrusted to me as her father. I
spent hours holding her and talking to her; I took her with
me on walks around the block and on trips across town. I
began to get up at 6:00 A.M. for her, and I even changed her
diapers. There was healing for the confusion I'd felt about
how my own father reacted to me as a child.

As a wife, knowledge of your husband's background can
prevent you from criticizing him. None of us needs condemnation, and your husband may need healing. I encourage you to
also allow your husband the freedom to create "first experiences" with your children. Both he and they will benefit.

A Sense of Playfulness

The playfulness that men feel as dads is the positive counterpart to the negative feeling of being forgotten or left out.

Nancy tells the story of a young couple at her church who
had recently adopted twins. The next Sunday during the
church service, the pastor wanted to recognize the new family, and so he asked the proud parents to stand.

There was a loud "whoop" from the back of the building,
and everyone turned to look at them standing, each one
holding one of the babies. But then the father did a curious
thing. In his excitement, he raised his daughter above his
head and pushed her up as high as he could in one quick
motion. What he had forgotten was that they were sitting
beneath the balcony overhang, and he had thrust his new
daughter up within inches of a wooden support beam.
Nancy still remembers the look on his wife's face and the
audible gasp from the rest of the congregation.

This father was giving expression to the sense of playfulness released in him by becoming a dad. It was partly that
same playfulness that sent me on the wild wagon ride with

my daughters that I described in chapter 1. But playfulness doesn't have to be so dangerous. It can be that little romp on the living room carpet. It can be a bucking bronco ride on Dad's back as he carts your son off to bed. It can be Dad holding his child upside down by the ankles while planting a raspberry on her bare belly. Kids love it. So do dads. "Rough-housing" is what Dee calls it.

Even as the children grow, your husband will probably remain playful, though the games he plays will change as your child grows. At times, playfulness may evolve into downright competitiveness, where your husband gives your child his first tastes of challenge. I suspect what's at work in your husband is a sense that "at least now for a while I can win; there'll be a time when I can't." I still remember that episode of "The Cosby Show" when the son, Theo, finally beats his dad in a game of one-on-one basketball. Those are big moments.

A Sense of Protection

Your adult son or daughter calls home and announces, "Dad, I've just been in an accident. I smashed my car up pretty bad."

It's nice to hear this as a father's immediate response: "Are *you* all right? . . . You sure? You didn't get scraped up or anything? . . . Good, I'm glad."

But sometimes this isn't the immediate response. Sometimes you're listening on the other extension, and he asks, "So, does the other driver have insurance? Did anyone get a ticket?"

This might not be his *first* question, but maybe it seems to you to be too quickly his *second* one.

Is the father who says this being callous and uncaring?

Possibly. But it's equally possible that he's giving expression to the distinct way men normally exercise protection.

Studies have been done on the different ways men and women grieve over the loss of a child. For mothers, the grief was immediate and intense. Men were more likely to put off the grieving for the moment, to say, "Well, let's get on with our lives." But men will revisit that grief later, and it will be just as painful and intense.[11] The danger is that the husband will consider the wife to be helpless and cowardly, while the wife will consider the husband to be callous and cold-hearted. Neither is necessarily true.

The protection that you as a mother bring to your children in a crisis is more than likely to be personal and emotional. You focus on the *person* of your child, and quickly begin to bind whatever wounds (physical or emotional) he or she might have suffered. A father's focus, on the other hand, is more likely to center on the *world* of your child. ("Can his car be repaired as soon as possible so that his world will be back to normal?") Both of you have your child firmly and benevolently in mind, and both of you are attempting to restore what was lost; you are simply dividing the labor and working well as a parenting team. I suspect if we had been down in Homestead, Florida, in the immediate aftermath of Hurricane Andrew, we would have seen many mothers consoling their children under the tin roofs that their fathers had just nailed above them. It will take fathers and mothers working together to restore the families of that community.

When a man becomes a father, a sense of protectiveness wells up within him to encompass his child and all his child's world. He even becomes more careful about himself—his child's father. One man writes, "I became aware, when Mary was pregnant, that I no longer had any right to die. . . . I stopped taking such huge risks. I found myself driving slower, avoiding rougher areas of town, actually listening to a life insurance salesman. . . . All for the reason that I was now important to this little thing, and I couldn't die because he needed me."[12]

One other particular way this protectiveness expresses itself in a father seems to be a concern that his children get fair treatment from others—from teachers, from coaches, from club leaders. It's another way of protecting a child's world, trying to make it as just and as fair as possible. In particular, he's afraid that others might not understand his kids as well as he does. We can look at this sense of protectiveness as the positive counterpart to a father's feelings of inadequacy described earlier.

A Concern for the Next Generation

If you were in your late twenties or early thirties before you had kids, you may have been teased about your "biological clock." Women, so they say, feel the need to bear children and start a family at that time in their lives. The male counterpart to that may be what I call a "generational clock." It hits when a father is in his forties or fifties, when he begins to be more reflective about what he has accomplished and especially what part of his life will be passed on to future generations.

It's the flip side of the negative emotion of feeling alone, a larger social concern growing out of the knowledge that his children and grandchildren will be around after he is gone; they'll be living in a world he helped to create.

This concern for the next generation will increase markedly as a father ages and his children grow up and begin to have children of their own. He'll begin to reflect, "What's it going to look like for them? Will they have it as good as I have had it?" and more important, "Are my children going to perpetuate the same values and ideals I gave to them? Are they going to carry on?"

Trueman Bliss was a venerable gentleman who was highly respected by his children and grandchildren. Throughout his life, Trueman wasn't noted for his long visits. Though he stopped frequently to see his grown sons and daughters in northern Michigan, Virginia, and Kansas, unless his kids could think up some project he would surely volunteer to help with (re-roof the house, pour cement, etc.), Trueman would soon be off to the next stop.

Trueman and his wife were "snowbirds" who left their Michigan home each winter to settle down near Sarasota, Florida. One November they packed up to head south and, as usual, swung up to northern Michigan to see their youngest son and his family. They stayed for just a day before driving all the way to Kansas to visit another son's family. Again, within two days, they were gone. They drove across to Virginia for another short visit, before going to Florida.

The visits that year were the shortest ever, so short that the sons and daughters wondered, "What's the hurry and what's the point? Why drive so far out of your way if you are only going to visit for a moment?" But then one of Trueman's daughters-in-law remembered overhearing something he'd said to his wife shortly before they left Kansas. He told her, "Well, everything looks okay here."

Just one week after arriving in Florida, Trueman had his second major heart attack, setting in motion the heart failure that would finally end his life. Maybe he had a subconscious premonition that his remaining days were short. He made it a point to visit his family one more time, not so much to say good-bye as to make sure that "everything looks okay here."

Fathers are like that.

The Proud Papa

Among the other cultural icons I've mentioned, we shouldn't forget this one (however outdated it might be): the man in the waiting room, receiving the news, "Mr. Smith, your wife has just had a girl!" Suddenly, the proud papa is laughing out loud, shaking hands with total strangers, distributing cigars to anyone who looks like they might smoke.

This may well be the same man who jumps to his feet in the bleachers while his son rounds third base. "That's my boy," he yells. The boy flushes in embarrassment. The bystanders smirk.

One of the most profound emotions a man feels in being a father is pride.

Recently, I spoke at a small men's breakfast at a church in Whiting, Kansas. Of the five men who attended the breakfast, one was an older man whose only son was killed in the Vietnam War. His son was the only Kansan to receive the Congressional Medal of Honor in that war. Tears glistened in this man's eyes as he told me about his son, and he invited me back to his home to see his son's medals and newspaper clippings and watch a video of his son's memorial ceremony. He was proud, very proud of his boy and the boy's bravery.

Men tend to take a sense of ownership in their children's accomplishments, which also explains why a man may get embarrassed when they fail. Your husband probably delights when your children succeed. In fact, if he is like most men, he wants them to actually *exceed* him in something. Not in everything, mind you—men can be competitive even with their kids—but nonetheless, a father takes pleasure when his children reach a higher level of achievement. How often have you heard it, especially in immigrant families: "I wanted opportunities for you that never existed for me. I wanted you to do what I never got the chance to do." Such pride becomes a powerful motivator for a father.

No doubt, you as a mother also delight when your children excel. But I believe there are some differences in emphasis to keep in mind.

Linda Wertheimer is a political correspondent for National Public Radio. One day, she brought her mother along to watch her work on Capitol Hill. Later Wertheimer commented on her mother's visit:

> I thought she would be impressed by the fact that members of Congress knew me by my first name, that I could call Senators off the floor and ask them questions, that I was very aggressive about getting what I wanted. But at the end of the day—no, she didn't even wait until the end of the day—Mother turned to me and said, "I didn't bring you up to talk to people like that."[13]

If Wertheimer's father had been the visitor, he might have been impressed with all the accomplishments that his daughter cited. No doubt, this mother was also impressed, but for her, appearance was at least as important as achievement. This mother placed significance on "manners," in the sense of the *way* achievements are arrived at, or in how their children *personally* come across. Fathers may tend to place more emphasis on achievement—the results—rather than appearance. A few years ago when the Chicago White Sox baseball team was first managing to put together a new winning tradition, the players came up with a slogan: "Winning

Ugly." They didn't look good doing it, and sometimes they didn't deserve it, but they were winning.

Keep your eyes open also to another possible difference between your husband and yourself when it comes to pride in your kids. When your child succeeds, your delight may be localized in what that accomplishment means for your child personally. Meanwhile, your husband may be taking greater delight in how that accomplishment *benefits the clan.* We must not forget an important cultural fact, namely that (for most families) your children bear your husband's name. When your son steps up to the batter's box or your daughter dances out on stage, your husband's name is at stake. Somewhere deep inside he feels this. His children are his posterity, what he leaves to the world. "How will I be remembered?" he asks. Well, the answer is right before him, playing on the living room floor at his feet.

Understanding the particulars of a father's pride can benefit you greatly as you seek to encourage your husband. Some of the gravest wounds you can inflict on a man are when you see your children misbehaving or failing in a particular task, and comment to your husband, "They are just like you." But when you save that comment for the moments when the children are reflecting one of your husband's virtues, then you have paid your husband one of the compliments he most longs to hear: "I see a lot of you in our children."

Fathering is a complex task, partly, I believe, because fathers are complex people. Your husband may or may not experience these positive and negative emotions; he may feel other things. He may be motivated by the positive, and dauntless in the face of the negative. Or he may be paralyzed by the negative, and simply nostalgic about the positive. He is his own man; no two fathers will be alike.

Your great challenge is to understand this man, your husband.

Questions for Personal Reflection

Think about these before discussion group.

1. Are there any *other* negative emotions your husband demonstrates as a father?

2. How does he feel about his own father?

3. How does he feel about his shortcomings as a father?

Questions for Discussion

To discuss with a small group

1. What positive comments have you heard your husband make about his fathering?

2. What feelings has he expressed to you or to others about his children?

3. Why is it important for your husband to express his feelings as a father?

5 What Your Husband *Does* as a Father

I never really respected what my father did for a living while I was at home. We lived in Wichita, and he worked for Beech Aircraft. He was a technician and apparently highly skilled; Beech would occasionally send him out to trouble-shoot electronic problems on aircraft all over the country. But in my mind, he was just an hourly factory worker.

I was in high school and had begun to run with a crowd from the other side of the tracks—the better side. I think now it intimidated my father to see me let off in front of our house in my friend's Mercedes Benz. Although our needs were met, my dad didn't make a great deal of money.

One day I arrived home from a long weekend with my rich friends. Dad was waiting for me, and we got into a conversation that disintegrated into an argument. Finally he said, "I bet you think I'm just a dumb factory worker."

I turned to him, stared him in the eyes, and with all my teenage insolence, I told him: "That's right; you're just a dumb factory worker."

He turned away. And remained away.

In the years that followed, I forgot the incident. But God did not, and he began to make some major changes in my life. He brought me to faith in Jesus Christ. He gave me a godly wife who bore me one child, then two, then three, four, five. Suddenly I was the father of five children—and a *concerned* father, not only for my own sake, but for the sake of all fathers out there. Suddenly, this man who did so little to honor his own dad had founded the National Center for Fathering.

"I don't understand it," my mother told me a few years back. "Your dad doesn't seem at all interested in what you do." He had never asked about the National Center for Fathering or the research I did. I guess she had even given him copies of magazine articles I had written on fathering, but he didn't read them. He didn't seem interested in what I did at work, or apparently at home for that matter. Although my family (including five of his grandkids) lives just two hours north of Wichita, Dad had only been up to visit twice in the past ten years, and he stayed only for the afternoon when he came.

It was during this time that the Lord suddenly brought the incident of my "dumb factory worker" insult back to mind. I realized that the heavenly Father wanted me to apologize to my earthly father. So the next time I had the opportunity, I resolved to make things right with him.

Dad and I went for a drive through the city streets, and it seemed like old times. He was driving; I was in the passenger seat; we talked about recent development projects and the future prospects of the city. We stopped to look at something, and that's when I spoke.

I asked him if he remembered when I called him a dumb factory worker. He stared out his side of the window and mumbled, "Not really," letting me know that, yes, he did.

"Dad," I said, "I distinctly remember that when I called you that, there was a hurt look in your eyes. And I want you to know that I'm sorry. I'm really sorry I did that."

He still didn't look back at me. "Oh, that's okay," he said. "That's in the past. We just have to forget about those things."

We talked some more, and the conversation on the subject slowly died out. We decided to drive on. His hand went to the ignition, his eyes stared out ahead, but then he slowly turned to me, looked me straight in the eyes, and asked me: "By the way, what do you do?"

I could barely answer him. I knew I was forgiven.

A Father's Job Description

One of the greatest things you can do for your husband is to understand and appreciate what he *does* as a father. Just as my dad may not have made as much money as my friends' fathers, so your husband might not be as good with the kids as your neighbor's husband. Maybe that man next door coaches Little League, serves on the PTA, and spends his Saturdays at home.

Be careful about comparisons, though. You might end up like the woman described by Gary Smalley and John Trent: She is curious about the couple who has just moved in across the street. Nearly every day, she watches the husband come home with a bouquet of flowers, a box of candy, or some other small gift. He meets his wife at the door and gives her a long hug and kiss.

After weeks of this, she finally confronts her husband as he walks in the door: "Have you ever noticed what our neighbor does to his wife every day when he comes home?"

"No, dear," her husband mumbles. "I haven't noticed."

So she describes the scene for him, and asks, "How come *you* don't ever do that?"

He looks at her, confused. "Honey, I can't do that," he replies. "I hardly know the woman!"[1]

Do you understand and appreciate what *your* husband does? Do you identify and recognize those things he does

Encouraging Your Husband in His Fathering Role

Over 2,000 fathers were asked to rate their satisfaction with the way their wives encourage them as fathers. Their responses can be grouped in the following ways:

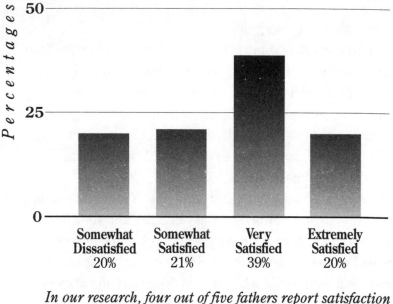

In our research, four out of five fathers report satisfaction with their wives' support of them in their fathering role.

right, however small those things might be (or might appear to you to be)?

The real place to begin is with a larger vision than just your husband (or your neighbor's husband); begin with trying to understand *fatherhood.* However well or however poorly you think your husband executes his job as a dad, however much or little you think he does as a father, do you understand and value the profession of fatherhood? Have you ever thought about your husband's job description as a father? It is what he aspires to, or falls short of, or feels the pressures of, or seeks recognition for, or finds victory through, or suffers defeat in. This "job description" controls a lot of what he does and molds a lot of who he is. If you understand fatherhood, you understand more about your husband, the father.

In the previous chapter we looked at the feelings involved in fathering. Now, let's look at fathering tasks.

There are two ways to perceive your husband's profession, fatherhood. One is the old way: that fathers are like assembly line workers who mindlessly put in their hours to draw their modest paychecks. The other perspective is a new way, infused with grace: Fathers are like highly skilled technicians, necessary for the proper functioning of a family. Same man. Same tasks. But a new perspective, a new calling.

Fatherhood through the Ages: The Four Ps

Certainly, fathering is not a recent invention, nor is scholarship about fatherhood. The Puritans were prolific writers on the subject. Two works, Aires's *Centuries of Childhood* and Goodsell's *The Family as a Social and Educational Institution,* specifically outline the historic tasks that fathers were expected to perform. These tasks can be summarized into what I call the four *P*s: A father was expected to (1) *protect* his children from the dangers of the world, (2) *provide* for their well-being by giving moral oversight and physical essentials, (3) *punish* his children for inappropriate behaviors, and (4) be a *progenitor* for his clan.

A father was expected to protect his children. Dangers in the form of wolves, horse thieves, and marauding Indians lurked in the world of our forefathers. Police forces and militia were small and scattered, and children depended on their

father's strength and bravery. They saw the rifle hanging
over the mantelpiece; they may have even seen their father
use it.

Children were also aware of how their fathers provided.
Provision is the second *P,* the second historical task of a
man. It's actually a biblical mandate: the Scriptures liken a
man who is not a trusty provider to being "worse than an
unbeliever" (1 Timothy 5:8). So our fathers worked out
among the merchants, and they came home with silver coins
for the coffers or a dressed-out goose for the supper table.
Or they went out to the fields with mules and plows, and har-
vested the grain, and slaughtered the hogs, and hunted the
game. When the Industrial Revolution came, and the factory
whistle blew, they heeded that call, too.

Our early fathers had a very broad view of provision.
They sought to provide the child with everything that the
child needed to function in the world, not just with food and
clothing. So fathers provided an education, too. In colonial
Massachusetts, it was a law that a father had to teach his children to read.[2]

The third historic task of a father was to *punish* his children when necessary. *Discipline* is of course a better word
(though it doesn't begin with *p),* because our early fathers
saw punishment as a means of disciplining or training their
children in good moral behavior. It was a function of the
father's educational role. Society left the discipline of juve-
niles to the father. He was supposed to administer specific
punishment for any crimes committed by the children. He
was responsible for any damages his children caused.

Finally, a father was expected to be a *progenitor* for his
clan. Preachers of the day would point to Malachi 2:15 and
claim that one of the primary purposes of being married is
to have "godly offspring" (NIV). And offspring they had.

Being procreative was implicit in the job description of being a father. When physical children were not possible, men were encouraged to become surrogate fathers to other children in the community.[3]

The Four Ps and Old Testament Laws

What do you think of the four *P*s? Would you be satisfied if your husband was only a good protector, provider, punisher, and progenitor? The four *P*s served their generation well, but over the years those tasks have changed to such a degree that if a father today is simply a good provider or disciplinarian he might well be accused of being "just an ordinary factory worker," someone who mindlessly does what he has to do without any vision for advancing the organization.

The Puritans saw the four historic tasks in the context of close involvement and relationship with their children. The four *P*s were very visible signs of their love and concern. Today, a father can perform the four *P*s without his children even noticing. In fact, he can do most of them without even being present. For example, today's father still protects his children, but mainly by paying taxes to support a police force and a military. When's the last time your children saw their dad shoot a charging grizzly bear? And of course your husband provides, but what he brings home is a little slip of paper called a paycheck. (With direct deposit, it might even be just a blip on a bank's computer screen.) A dressed-out steer is much more impressive. Through child support payments, a divorced father can provide for his children without ever seeing them.

If anything, in the past few decades, the role of punisher has become one of the father's two more conspicuous main roles as assigned by our culture (provider being the other).

The father is the disciplinarian of last resort; his children are told, "Just wait till your dad comes home." And finally, the role of progenitor has almost been rendered superfluous, at least in the historic sense of propagating the clan and carrying on a line of descent. Women can be impregnated at sperm banks, and when there *is* a father present, the increasing mobility of so many families is rapidly decreasing the sense of the clan or extended family. The patriarch (like the matriarch) gets honored only at the ceremony of a fifieth wedding anniversary.

If you think of fatherhood just in terms of the four traditional tasks, or the four *P*s, then you are in danger of conveying to your husband that you think of him as just an ordinary factory worker, still plugging away on mindless mechanics, as outdated in this computer age as an early Henry Ford assembly line.

Another analogy might be helpful, that of the Old Covenant given to God's chosen people. The Old Covenant was good and served its purpose well. It marked a special relationship: God entering into covenant with his people, calling himself their God. The covenant detailed the tasks of a good Hebrew and protected them from the moral destruction that plagued other families. Over the years, though, the Hebrews began to lose sight of the relationship behind the covenant and began to focus on the mechanics. The Old Covenant wanted them to *be* something (holy as God is holy), but the Pharisees and others wanted to *do* something instead: keep meticulous laws. It was time for a New Covenant.

There's a new covenant that today's fathers are making with their children. They are reinforcing and extending the four *P*s with what we at the National Center call the four I-CANs.

The I-CANs: Marks of a Skilled Technician

Times are changing, and so are fathers. So are the things fathers are allowed and expected to do.

Judd and Nancy Swihart demonstrate this. When their oldest son, Derrick, was about to be delivered, the doctor made Judd say good-bye to Nancy at the swinging doors to the labor room. The doctor said to Judd, "You may as well go home now. I'll call you when everything is over."

Fifteen months later, in a different state and with a different doctor, Judd was allowed to spend some time with Nancy during labor, but again was sent away, this time to the waiting room with all the other nervous fathers, to await the arrival of their second son, Daniel.

It wasn't until Sara was born, several years later, that Judd was finally allowed into the delivery room. At the last minute the doctor, not their regular physician, gave Judd permission to don the green hospital garb and stand by the door to watch the miracle of birth, the same miracle that Nancy had witnessed alone twice before. How fortunate are fathers now to be a welcome and integral part of this indescribable birthing process.

Judd and Nancy's three-part story demonstrates how society has changed; fathers are now invited to participate in more and more of the whole wonderful range of parenting, well beyond their four historic tasks.

It's not just a case of being expected to do more (though I believe this is true). It's a reintroduction of *relationship* into the whole fathering equation. For example, Lamaze classes are more than just another meeting to attend. Coaching the wife is more than just another skill to acquire. Being present in the delivery room represents an opportunity to be involved in a child's life from the very beginning. Martin

Greenberg uses the term *engrossment* to explain a father's feelings during the birthing experience.[4] More than your husband's body is engaged: His whole soul is *engrossed* in this joyous moment.

Fathers still ask the National Center, "What do I do? Tell me what I need to do." But they aren't asking those questions merely to check items off their list and "fulfill their obligation to society." Invariably, the questions are: "What do I do to be a *better* dad?" or "Tell me what I need to do to be *closer* to my children."

It's strange, but at the same time our country is experiencing a tragic wave of fatherlessness, it is also experiencing a fathering renaissance among those who are even mildly committed to the task. In some segments of society, and especially in the church, more and more homes are resounding with "Daddy's home!" and finding that the man walking through the front door is different than the man who preceded him.

In our analogy, society has begun to perceive fathers not as "ordinary factory workers," but as men with the potential to become highly skilled technicians who are dedicated to excellence in their work. They care about the people they serve (their children). They care about the family and how it prospers or suffers. They acquire new skills and build networks of support.

In our other analogy, the new perspective on fatherhood is like the establishing of the New Covenant. In the New Covenant, God emphasized relationship; we can know him through Jesus Christ. He introduced a new motivation: love instead of obligation. He let people know that he is more concerned with who they are than with what they do. He wrote the laws on tablets of flesh (their hearts), not on tablets of stone. Many of the same tasks and laws were still commanded by God (don't murder, don't steal, don't commit adultery, etc.), and those who were wise still obeyed these laws, but the context changed. In grace, God's people began to carry out those tasks because those tasks pleased God and fostered their relationship with him. Similarly, for our new breed of fathers the old tasks (including the four *P*s) become expressions of the *relationship,* and not ends in themselves.

Have you noticed these changes in your husband? Have you at least seen them in society? If not, our hope is that this book will equip you to be a catalyst for that change.

If there is such a thing as the "new father," the question remains: What does this new father *do*? What's the job description? I think in many ways it's still being written. Let me share with you the first draft. It's called the I-CANs, an acronym for the four major fathering dimensions. They are designed to provide direction. In a moment of doubt, his head on the pillow, his eyes staring at the ceiling, your husband sighs. "Being a father seems so much more complex than when my dad did it," he says. "*Can I* be a good father?"

Your response can be "Yes, you can!" Your husband can be an Involved, Consistent, Aware, and Nurturant father. Let me explain how we came up with these qualities.

Five years ago, I and a team of four scholars (Nancy's husband was one of them) set out to find ways to help fathers. We knew that for a variety of reasons, many fathers today feel confused about their role. Many of them had fathers who were not positive models, and when their first child is born, they wrestle with many questions of how they should be performing in this new and very permanent role. Our research team spent much time reviewing all the current research on fathering; we also developed profiles of over five thousand fathers. We struggled to understand how the old

covenant of fathering tasks needed to be reshaped so that
fathers could understand their new tasks.

We compiled a long, elaborate list of tasks that fathers do
perform, or *should* perform, to benefit their children. Examples include involvement in education, involvement in discipline, spiritual equipping, allowing freedom of expression,
and knowing their children. It read like a list of Old Testa-
ment laws.

Through factorial analysis and other research methods,
we discovered there were four overarching principles of
fathering which together seemed to encompass all that a
father did. They were more accurately traits or characteristics of fathering, rather than actions, but when they
were applied to each of the activities, they told a man how to
be an effective dad.

The four dimensions of fathering are *I*nvolvement, *C*onsis-
tency, *A*wareness, and *N*urturance. We labelled them the I-
CANs. Fathers who have attended National Center for
Fathering seminars consistently report that the I-CANs have
been the most helpful information to them.

If you understand these four principles, you'll understand
what your husband is attempting as he seeks to become a
better dad.

Involvement

The first of the I-CANs is Involvement. This encompasses
how much time, structured and unstructured, a dad spends
with his children, and also the degree to which he participates in their lives. He may spend one hour alone with the
children at night, but if he's reading the newspaper, his level
of involvement with the children is probably not very high!

Our society is growing more aware of how important it is

A Wife's Encouragement Affects
Her Husband's Involvement as a Father

Over 1,500 fathers were asked to rate their satisfaction level with their wives' support of their fathering. Fathers were asked to describe themselves as being dissatisfied (LOW), having mixed feelings (MED) or being satisfied (HIGH) with the support given to them by their wives. These three groups of fathers were then compared in their **Involvement,** *as measured by the Personal Fathering Profile. The differences in the scores from each group are as follows:*

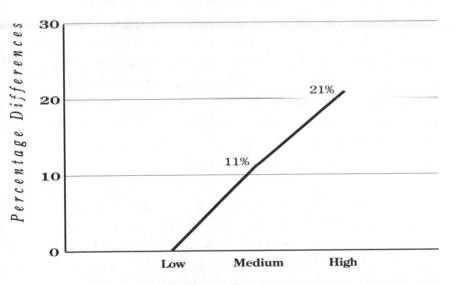

The more a husband senses your support of him as a father, the more likely it is that he will be highly involved in the lives of his children.

Involvement measures to what degree a father participates in his child's life. This could include playing or working with the child, attending the child's activities, tending to daily routines, or just spending unstructured time with the child. The father is engaged in the life of the child.

for a father to be involved on more than a superficial level. We now know that children benefit in so many different ways when the father participates in their lives. The children have a sense of independence, more social abilities, confidence, flexibility, better intellectual development, and greater compassion.[5] It's good to see more fathers changing diapers, helping with homework, and even rearranging their work schedules to make time for the kids. Fathers are making some giant steps!

We all know, however, that a father's involvement is much more than merely being there for the child's birth, or sitting in the stands at the softball games. Dads need to spend time with their children on a daily basis: They need to get down on the floor and wrestle with them, schedule special times to eat out alone with each one, watch movies with their daughters, listen to their kids' music, and join the family discussions around the dinner table. When you see this happening, give some good feedback to your husband. Let your husband know what a positive effect he is having on his children.

One of the most important and necessary gifts any father can give to his child is himself. Your husband's involvement in your children's lives in a healthy and regular way will give your children a clear sense of belonging and purpose rather than the feelings of abandonment, helplessness, and confusion that are brought about by physically or emotionally absent fathers. Involvement is the lifeblood of parenting, and especially of fathering.

We have all heard the big debate over which is most important: quality time or quantity time. I believe that *without* quantity time with a child, it is very difficult to bring about genuine *quality* time. Both are important, and in fact, one will often lead to the other.

Quality time depends upon an established relationship which is built on trust. And it takes lots of time to develop that trust with a child. Children can tell when they're being forced into meaningful time, as if their father could cue up quality time like a video tape and turn it on to fit into his schedule. But nobody is fooled! Likewise, time by itself is not enough. Children need their father to be available to spend time with them, but they also realize when he is there in body but not in spirit. He needs to be accessible to them at the same time that he is available. What does this look like? It means no newspaper during conversations; it means looking them in the eyes and actually listening; it means getting down on the floor with them instead of watching them. It means investing his energies into their lives.

Consistency

We all need people in our lives to respond to us in a consistent manner. For children, experiencing a dad who is consistent and predictable is crucial. A father who is consistent maintains a certain level of predictability. The kids know what he is going to say about the dog being in the house. They know that when he looks at them in a certain way, he means business. They know that he will always lead in prayer before the meal. They know that when he tells them something it is the truth. Children need that source of security, a fixed point from which to explore the world, and parents, especially fathers, are those reference points.

The advantages of consistent parenting have been verified by research that has been done on adolescents. The sons of consistent parents were basically well adjusted and intellectually oriented, and they had stable relationships with others. The daughters showed more self-assurance and vitality,

A Wife's Encouragement Affects Her Husband's Consistency as a Father

*Over 1,500 fathers were asked to rate their satisfaction
level with their wives' support of their fathering. Fathers
were asked to describe themselves as being dissatisfied
(LOW), having mixed feelings (MED) or being satisfied
(HIGH) with the support given to them by their wives.
These three groups of fathers were then compared in their
Consistency as a father, as measured by the Personal
Fathering Profile. The differences in the scores from each
group are as follows:*

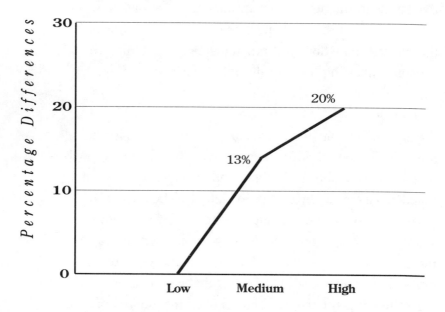

*The more a husband senses your support of him as a
father, the more likely it is that he will be consistent in
his fathering tasks.*

*Consistency is shown in a father's predictability. He
maintains a certain level of regularity both in his personal characteristics and in his fathering habits. People
around him know what to expect from him.*

were less anxious, and didn't fit into stereotypes.[6] Often it takes years of consistent parenting to enjoy the positive impact on our children, but it's well worth the wait.

When your husband is a stable and reliable anchor, your children will be able to survive the storms going on around them . . . and inside them as well. It's easy to see the effect inconsistency has on your children if they are never sure where their father stands or how he will react in a situation. They are left to be tossed about by every wind or wave that arises. Certainly all people go through storms, but consistency is a way of making sure all the hatches are tight, the sails are pulled in, the ship is secure.

Sadly enough, consistency is lacking in many of our American households. Not only are children wary of what will happen when they walk through the door after school, but consistency is often lacking even in the simple areas: the regularity of meals, having clean clothes, going to bed on a regular schedule, and having an opportunity for regular and open expression of feelings and ideas. These are areas that provide great comfort for children, and in this age of rapid movement and busyness, it takes both parents to consciously make sure some level of consistency marks their homes.

Tied up with consistency is also the conviction with which a parent operates. Dads have a big role in this area. If he says he stands for something, does he waver under stress, under temptation, under scrutiny? Do your kids know what their father will do when he sees the TV show getting too "mature" and suggestive? When they walk in the door and announce that they've done a little cosmetic alteration to the side of the Chevy? Do they know how he'll react when they strike out, or fail a class, or get caught in a lie? Children of consistent fathers do.

A father who is truly consistent will be one who has determined to be an effective father even in the face of hardship. He will work hard in his fathering role even when it costs or when he has to put forth extra effort.

You can help your husband be consistent by being consistent yourself, and also by noticing the little things he does that are predictable and positive. Notice the effort that he makes to control his temper and to respond with gentleness every time the children get in a skirmish. Thank him for trying to work his schedule so that he is home at a decent time for dinner every evening. Support him when he turns off the suggestive television show. Your efforts will be rewarded as you consistently encourage him to be consistent! And if he is consistent in the small things, it will help him to succeed in whatever larger challenges arise as he works at raising the future leaders of the twenty-first century, his own children.

Awareness

The third major area, awareness, has to do with a father's understanding of his children and their world. Some dads opt out and leave this area up to Mom. Life becomes too complicated, and they feel out of place, not included in the lives of their children. You can quickly tell if a father is aware or oblivious: Does he describe his daughter simply as "a good kid" or more elaborately as "a creative, outgoing overachiever who is always sensitive to the needs of those around her, who hates algebra and asparagus, and is the kind of child who likes to learn things through her own experiences"? An aware father will know what events are occurring in his child's life. He knows about the child's growth needs and personal characteristics. But he also reaches a balance between being intrusive (too involved) in his child's life on one side, and being totally oblivious on the other side.

There are two types of awareness—*general* and *specific*—and both are important. General awareness is knowing what to expect from a child at a particular stage in her development and anticipating potential tensions and problems that tend to come with that age level. Your local library will have materials that can help your husband prepare for the "terrible twos" or the dreaded teenage years, and there are many other reliable sources around him every day . . . such as other fathers, and you! It is especially reassuring for you to know you can give your husband information that he may need. But your spirit, your tone of voice, and your attitude will play an important role in how he receives that information. Some wise husbands take advantage of the great parenting resource their wives provide, and others may look elsewhere. Examine your own desire to offer advice, and be sensitive to your husband's willingness to accept it.

Specific awareness tells your husband about the unique character traits of his children. He gains this information by being involved with his kids and, again, by talking with you. You give your husband a more complete picture of your children because you have your own perspective on them, and your own way of relating to them. What does he know about his daughter's best friend? What important life event is his son passing through, and how will he react? What are his children's dreams? Their biggest disappointments?

In the 1992 summer Olympic games, British runner Derek Redmond pulled a muscle coming around the last turn of his race. As the other competitors left him behind, he continued to hobble toward the finish line, his face grimacing with pain. Soon his father appeared at his side, put his arm around his son, brought him under control, and then continued with him toward the finish line. The father must have known that the best thing for his son's leg would be to get him to sit down and seek immediate treatment, and he surely could have forced him off the track. But this father knew his son. He'd been watching him during the past four years, knew how much time the son had given up to train for this one day, and he knew that his son had come to Barcelona for one reason: to finish this race. It was important to his son, and he was doing his part to help him achieve his goal.

Nurturance

The last basic area where your husband needs strength is nurturance. Nurturance is the ability to respond to the emotional needs of his children. As you probably know, most fathers struggle with this. Some children rarely hear their father say, "I love you. I'm proud you're my daughter," or "I'm proud you're my son." Often such words are uttered only during a major sickness, or even on the father's deathbed. You need to impress upon your husband that that's much too late. Many a well-meaning mother tries to help an emotionally crippled dad by saying to her children, "Your father loves you. Look how hard he works to provide and care for you." But there's really no substitute for words of love and affirmation spoken regularly by fathers to their children.

In the movie *The Great Santini,* Robert Duvall plays a rather involved, consistent, and aware military father. But one weakness of Duvall's character is that he is not nurturant. In several scenes of the movie, the children are hungry for a listening ear, an affirming word or an affectionate touch, but the tough father restrains himself and never gives in. He simply goes on doing his business and has little to do with the emotional side of his children. Maybe this, to some degree, explains much of what many wives are seeing in their husbands. They were never nurtured by their fathers, and so they struggle with being nurturant. Yet it does not have to be that way.

A nurturant, encouraging father reaches out; he is proactive in offering affirmation or comfort; he takes the initiative in giving recognition. "In you I am well pleased," he communicates. He tapes the crudely colored crayon drawing on his office wall. He doesn't fly into a rage when a report card has mostly *B*s instead of *A*s. His discipline is done in gentleness and his criticism is never harsh.

A nurturant father is a rare commodity. You can help your husband learn to listen to your children, acknowledge their feelings, and then show his pride and love for them by nurturing them both physically and verbally. You help him by being an example, by giving him feedback, and by complimenting him and encouraging him when you see the good that he's doing.

Applying the I-CANs

It is remarkable how basic these fathering principles are. Despite his busy schedule, you *can* help your husband to be more involved in the lives of your children, more consistent in his behavior patterns, more aware of the events occurring in your kids' lives, and more committed to showing them verbal, emotional, and physical love. These dimensions of fathering—Involvement, Consistency, Awareness, and Nurturance—simplify the fathering process. They do not provide a surefire fathering formula; there's no such thing. Instead, the I-CANs are a framework for understanding.

Fathering is a big task for your husband, and it will always carry a certain degree of uncertainty. The profound simplicity of the I-CANs of fathering, however, can be the handles that he needs to make the task manageable. He *can* become successful in the eyes of his children, and encouraging any sign of the I-CANs that you see manifested in his fathering may be an important step in that process.

Questions for Personal Reflection

Think about these before discussion group.

1. What tasks was your father responsible for while you were growing up?

2. Thinking about the I-CANs of fathering, which of these is your husband most proficient in? In which one does he need the most improvement?

3. Does your husband have a basic framework like the I-CANs to help him understand his fathering?

Questions for Discussion

To discuss with a small group

1. In past decades, how did fathers know whether or not they were doing a good job?

2. How do you feel about the "new" roles fathers are being called to fulfill?

3. Do the I-CANs of fathering also relate to mothering? How does a mother demonstrate I-CAN?

6 Obstacles Your Husband Faces as a Father

There are stones, pits, and potholes in your husband's path to effective fathering. It's easy to stumble.

By this point, a picture of your husband as a father is emerging in your mind. Maybe you've never taken time to glance beside you and observe this man who shares your family's yoke. What he does affects what you do, as together you rear your children into adulthood and godliness.

One way to consider what we've talked about so far is to think of the pressures your husband feels on his side of the yoke. In chapter 4 we talked about the five negative emotions or fears that your husband carries into fathering. These are internal pressures, like what an ox might feel in the natural strain and weariness of its muscle. In chapter 5, we talked about your husband's responsibilities as a father. These are divine pressures—God's job description for a dad—and might be compared to the road laid out before the ox, the distance it must travel.

In this chapter, we will talk about external pressures, those obstacles the world (or at least the world *in the 1990s*) places in front of your husband. These are stones in his path. Some of them, small but sharp and jagged, leave his feet bloody. Others are larger but unstable and can cause him to twist an ankle. Still others are huge and obstructive, so large that he stops in the yoke and wonders which way to turn.

As a wife, your job is *not* to remove these obstacles for

your husband, however much you might wish to. In fact, in our yokemate imagery, that would look quite silly: one oxen trying to strain out directly in front of the other, sweeping away the rubble in his path. The yoke just doesn't permit it, and the oxen would end up tripping over each other.

In some sense, all the pressures that we've mentioned are *divine* pressures. Our sovereign God knows what he's doing. Obstacles are trials that can yield growth. Eventually, by God's grace, your husband's feet toughen up, his muscles harden, and he ends up pulling his load with more strength and confidence than ever.

Your children also need to see their father encounter and overcome obstacles. One day (and it won't be long) they will encounter their own obstacles and crises. How well they overcome their problems may largely depend on what they've seen their father do. If he has modeled courage and endurance, then they too are encouraged to persevere. God knows what he's doing. A father's trials are often divinely orchestrated object lessons.

Glen Elder wrote a book entitled *Children of the Great Depression.* In particular, he was looking for how families were affected by the Depression of the 1930s. Elder found that adolescents from economically deprived homes came out of the Depression more capable of handling other crises than the adolescents whose families were relatively unaffected by the Depression. As he states: "However onerous the task may be, there is gratification and even personal growth to be gained in being challenged by a real undertaking if it is not excessive or exploitative."[1]

So, you are not responsible for removing the obstacles that the world places before your husband. You are not even necessarily responsible for relieving the pressure of those obstacles. What you are responsible for, as a woman who loves her husband, is to understand who your husband is and what he experiences as a father. From there, God will show you what to do about the stones in your husband's path. (I suspect he'll lead you to concentrate on your husband—encouraging him—and not on the obstacles.)

The Greatest Barriers Fathers Face

As part of our research in 1991, the National Center for Fathering asked men, "What are the greatest barriers you face in being an effective dad?" The number one answer (27 percent) was "a lack of resources," namely the scarcity of time, money, and energy. The second answer (24 percent) involved personal character flaws like the father's own anger or impatience. The third answer (17 percent) was "a lack of know-how," or not possessing the necessary parental skills. (I believe these last two answers—character flaws and lack of skills—can be grouped together under the heading of a larger barrier: "lack of an effective fathering model while growing up." We discussed this briefly in chapter 4.)

The fourth answer (14 percent) dealt with outside forces which compete against the father for the attention and affection *of the children* (i.e. peer pressure, television, a child's busy schedule). The final answer (8 percent) was an "unsupportive relationship with my wife."

In chapter 4, we touched on a father's personal character flaws mainly through our discussion of the five negative fathering emotions. They can keep your husband from being the father he wants to be. In chapter 7, we will look at some ways wives hinder men in their fathering. In this chapter, we'll take up the remaining three answers that men gave to the question, "What are the greatest barriers you face in being an effective dad?" We'll look at a scarcity of resources,

an overwhelming explosion of knowledge, and a fierce struggle for the hearts of your children.

A Scarcity of Resources

There are only so many hours in the day, only so much
money in the checking account, only so much "oomph" left
in your husband's tired body at the end of the week. Effective fathering begins with commitment, and commitment is
a matter of investment. Like a depositor walking up to a
bank teller's window, each day your husband invests a little
something in your children's lives. He stoops to tie a shoe-
lace. He pays the electric bill. He reads a bedtime story. He
administers discipline. He pays a dental bill. He gives a hug.

Sometimes, though, your husband may feel like he's got
nothing left to invest. He stands at the teller's window, he
hears his children's needs clamoring in the background, but
he digs in his pockets, flips through his wallet, frantically pats
around his jacket. Nothing. No more time, energy, or money.

You as a mother no doubt feel the squeeze, too, especially
if you work outside the home. While the extra paycheck is
nice, you are probably discovering that what is credited to
the financial column is debited from the time and energy col-
umns. In the resource business, we often rob Peter to pay
Paul. Women are no strangers to the fact of scarcity.

I wonder, though, whether fathers don't feel the shortage
in a different way than mothers. For instance, if you had to
answer the question, "What is the greatest barrier you face
as a mother?" would you have listed "a lack of money, time,
and energy (particularly money)" as your number one
answer? Fathers did.

When God pronounced his curse after the fall of Adam
and Eve, he localized those curses in apparently specific

ways. For example, he addressed the serpent and told it, "You will crawl on your belly and you will eat dust all the days of your life" (Genesis 3:14, NIV). But he also addressed our parents. The Bible says specifically that he turned to one (Eve) and said one thing, and then to the other (Adam) to say another thing.

> To the woman He said, "I will greatly multiply your pain in childbirth, in pain you shall bring forth children; yet your desire shall be for your husband, and he shall rule over you" (3:16).
> Then to Adam He said, . . . Cursed is the ground because of you; in toil you shall eat of it all the days of your life. Both thorns and thistles it shall grow for you; and you shall eat the plants of the field; by the sweat of your face you shall eat bread, till you return to the ground, because from it you were taken." (3:17-19)

To the extent that these two distinct curses (Eve's and Adam's) are parallel, I think we can legitimately ask this question about your husband: Is it possible that your husband feels the pressure to provide for your children with the same degree of pain in his psyche that you felt in your body when you brought those children into the world?

It's a startling question, and I don't know how to answer it because I've never experienced labor (nor do I wish to). Nonetheless, with only a brief nod to the fact that the word *labor* can mean two things, I can definitely state this: Your husband feels *strongly* the pressure to make ends meet.

God did not say that work is a curse any more than he said that childbirth is a curse. Both are divinely ordained, and both yield beautiful results. It is the process which is painful. There are contracts and contractions, morning rush hours and morning sickness. With the curse placed on work, Adam was required to invest more energy and more time to yield the same results. At the same time, he had less energy and less time than he had before. He had to garnish energy from a body that had begun to decay. And while previously he had an unlimited pool of hours to work with (after all he was going to live forever), now suddenly God had placed a cap on his life called death. Suddenly, there were only so many hours in the day, so many days in the week, so many weeks in a lifetime. Adam entered the economy of scarcity that we, his children, have felt ever since.

Remember our earlier story of Stephen walking into the house past his daughter Bethany? She was waiting to be taken into his arms. He was searching for the couch. He had just finished a ten-hour shift at work.

Money. Money is definitely one of the resources in question. Today, unlike just a few decades ago, the majority of families depend on two incomes. You may be among those wives who contribute to the family coffers. In fact, it's possible that you may be bringing home a *larger* paycheck than your husband. And yet even so, I would venture to guess that your husband still feels the pressure of the *ultimate responsibility* of providing for his family. You might want to argue that he *shouldn't* feel that pressure, but that's not the point; it's likely he does.

Financial provision is one of the tasks of an effective father. Financial pressure is one of the curses. It is a stone that appears often in a father's path. Finances and fathering are not often separated.

Finances can weigh heavily even in a man's decision to

become a father. Last night, one of our directors was having dinner with a friend. The man's three-year-old son was also at the table.

"You know," our director said, "your first kid turned out so good. You guys should have another one."

"We can't afford it," his friend replied.

It's a common response.

I know a Christian man who has two children and is thinking of a third. "I feel guilty," he says. "I know that children are a blessing from God and that God provides, but Joan and I probably won't have a third child simply because I can't imagine how we can afford it."

It may seem cold and calculating to think of children in terms of the bottom line, but the pressure is real.

After all the children have arrived, finances and fathering link up again during the hard times. One recent study of African-American fathers showed a correlation between economic sufficiency and the level of active participation they had with their kids.[2] The more they were able to provide for their children's material needs, the more freedom they felt in providing for their emotional needs. In a study of job and income loss, fathers who responded irritably and with pessimism to a loss (certainly the natural thing to do) were more punitive and less nurturant in their interaction with their kids.[3] These men in both these studies seemed unable to separate their provision of resources from their work as a father.

Time and Energy. For most American families, though, perhaps yours included, the main obstacle posed by the pressure of finances is not "keeping body and soul together." It is the amount of scarce resources we are forced to invest in bringing home a paycheck. We expend time and energy outside the home. Work produces, but work also consumes. Unless priorities are established and self-enforced, work can steal time and energy away from a man's family.

Last week I flew to Phoenix for business. Usually I try to bring my wife, Dee, and the kids in on my travel decisions, and usually I try to take one of my kids along with me on the trip. But for this trip, the flight was leaving on the same day the decision was made. I would only be gone overnight. Dee agreed that the trip was important, but my kids were ribbing me for taking off.

"Hey, it's part of the job. What do you want me to do, flip hamburgers at Kreem Kup?" I said, referring to a small corner diner a block from our house.

"You can't cook," my son Joel (a man of few words) replied.

I guess I'm stuck. But even as a fathering advocate I need to monitor my work demands in the same way that Dr. Don Burwell did. Don is a fathering advocate to the African-American community. He tells the story of a time in his life when he was traveling a lot. He called home one afternoon to talk to his family. His youngest daughter answered the phone, and Don greeted her with enthusiasm and asked her how her week was going. After they talked for several minutes, he said cheerfully, "Okay, honey. Now may I speak to Mommy?"

What he heard almost made him drop the receiver. His daughter set the phone down and called out, "Mommy, it's the invisible man on the phone." Needless to say, Don changed his priorities.

A Father's Greatest Resource: Himself. In the end, the answer to a father's lack of resources is not to acquire more resources, but to wisely manage and effectively prioritize the resources he has been given. Robert had a lot of resources. He was a doctor. His wife was an attorney. They were both busy people, and their son Jason was left to do pretty much whatever he pleased. And so he did. Jason's behavior worsened until one day he dumped a gallon of paint into the swimming pool, causing considerable damage.

Unable to put up with his behavior any longer, the parents sent him for therapy. Robert sent a note to the therapist saying, "Tell Jason he can have anything he wants if he'll just stop his terrible behavior."

When the therapist asked Jason what he wanted, the boy knew he could have asked for any new electronic gadget, possibly even a car with a driver to take him around town.

His answer was short, clear and simple: "I want my father."

A man gives his children their father when he finally stops and asks, "What priority do I place on my family?" When he begins to order the rest of his life around those priorities, he may find reserves of resources for his children previously undiscovered. Dan was a fellow who loved to play golf, and he worked with others who loved to play golf. But one day, he turned down an offer. "Dave," he said, "I need to put off playing golf for a while. For this season of my life, I need the time, money, and energy for my kids."

I'll also tell you that effective fathers carry their family priority one step further. We found this out in our research on "Protection and Provision" for *The 7 Secrets of Effective Fathers.* Effective fathers don't really *subordinate* work priorities below family priorities; instead they *subsume* work priorities into the family priority. In other words, when they go to work they know *why* they are going there. It's not to put in their hours or to make money or to make a name for themselves; they go to work in order to provide for their families and thus fulfill one of their fathering functions. These men are consciously "being a dad" throughout the day, even while away from the home. Such a mind-set gives them wisdom in how to best invest their limited time, money, and energy.

Helping your husband to see the connection between work and fathering and then appreciating what he has done are vital steps in helping to bring him into the process of fathering.

A Lack of Know-How. Your husband might be like the other men we surveyed who said that "lack of know-how" is one of the major barriers they face as a father.

"Know-how" is important to a man. It's his surest ticket to advancement in the workplace, and he probably invests a lot in acquiring new skills and honing old ones. He's been enculturated to be task-oriented and skills-based. It's little wonder he's aware of a lack of parental skills.

Many men have confided to me that they are intimidated by their wives when it comes to parenting. "She's a natural," one man said. "I don't see how she does it. She always knows what to do."

Many men think you women have an instinctive knack for being a parent. Do you? I know many women who've worked hard at becoming a good mother. They've processed a painful past, they've studied parenting technique, they've built a solid support network of other women. The instinctive, intuitive mother who "always knows what to do" might be a stereotype, but the important point is that it is a stereotype held by many men—perhaps your husband as well. He may secretly feel intimidated by you.

Why do men perceive that they lack parenting know-how? Because they do, many of them. *Many fathers don't have a clue* when it comes to how to be a good dad. I think the major cause of this lack of know-how is the fact that many men grew up without present or effective fathers in their homes. God designed a training program for boys to learn how to be good dads. He intended fathers to teach their sons by modeling how to be involved, consistent, aware, and nurturant. The apprenticeship process short-circuited when the teachers skipped town.

The good news is that a father who lacked a fathering model can always find a new one. If your husband lacks know-how, he can still find it elsewhere. In the past two years, more books have been published specifically on fathering than during any other time I know of. There are great books on general parenting, many of which you have probably read and can recommend. There are older men who can teach your husband about being a dad. And of course you, his wife, can share with him what you know about being a parent.

The Explosion of Knowledge

To keep the theme centered on outside pressures (as opposed to internal ones), we can zero in on one way the world adds to a father's lack of know-how, namely through the explosion of knowledge.

Your husband probably senses that one of his responsibilities as a father is to help introduce his children to the world and effectively guide them through it. I joke often that the father's stock-in-trade is "the lecture," those moments when he boldly gathers the family around and imparts his wisdom from on high. After all, Hugh Beaumont used to climb the stairs to the boys' bedroom, sit on the corner of one of the beds, and sagely advise Wally and Beaver about how to

handle troubles at school. Bill Cosby took one of the Huxt-
able children into the kitchen for a glass of apple juice and a
lecture on the way things are. Robert Young proved "father
knows best."

But it's hard to "know best" when there is so much in the
world to know. In fact, a father can become overwhelmed at
the complexities of this age. How do you guide a child
through territory that is so new you never got to map it out
yourself? Here's how Nancy describes it for Judd and herself:

> At our house, we can't even pretend to know the
> answers to some of the problems our kids have
> brought home from school. Our children are the ones
> who taught us how to work the VCR and other elec-
> tronic devices. They set the clock in the car, they can
> name every make of car we pass on the road, and they
> speak fluently about math concepts I'm sure I never
> heard of. Most children these days learn more from
> their schools, from television, from their peers than
> they learn from their parents.

Her last statement is true. Children now apparently perceive fathers (and mothers) as incapable of teaching them
about the world. One study of teenagers claimed that in
1960, children were influenced the greatest by their parents,
then by teachers, their peers, and the church, in that order.
In 1980, the list put peers on the top, followed by parents,
media, and teachers.[4] Today, according to youth specialist
Walt Mueller, the list reads media, peers, parents, then teachers. "Media shapes peer culture," he says.[5] The subtle under-
lying message, as parents fall farther and farther down the
list, is, "Your old man is out of it."

Of course, a great deal of the pressure is illegitimate. Who cares if your kid can program the VCR faster than you can? But however shallow these skills might be, they are still skills, and it used to be a father who taught his children the skills they needed for living. I remember growing up in Wichita and seeing all the signs throughout town: "Classen and Sons Electric Company," "Chapman and Sons Family Grocers." Such signs are seldom seen anymore. They attest to a time when a man taught his son a trade.

The greater reason this pressure is illegitimate is that we have too often bought into our culture's myth that knowledge is the same thing as wisdom. An example: Your husband could scramble about attempting to acquire all the latest medical data about AIDS—how it's transmitted, how to prevent it—in an attempt to advise your children. Yet all that knowledge isn't really necessary; the best preventative is an old one: abstinence until marriage. The principles of sexual purity are not new; preventing AIDS is just one recent application of a moral principle your husband probably learned from his parents. His wisdom will benefit his children much more than his newfound knowledge. If you take care of the few "big" issues, you take care of many small problems in the process.

Granted, fathers should not be naive. They need to know what is going on in their children's world. There are books designed to inform parents what influences are shaping their children, and we recommend them (we're even publishing one, by Walt Mueller). But fathers need not feel overwhelmed. As a wife, you may have to occasionally remind your husband to relax. Tell him to trust the principles of wisdom that God has given. They are enough to guide your children even through the explosive 1990s.

Competition for Your Children

Dan Quayle had Murphy Brown as his media nemesis. I have Ice-T.

Ice-T is a popular rap musician who is the lead singer for "Body Count." I hate his lewd and violent lyrics; I hate even more his philosophy of life. He contributed an article to the July 1992 issue of *Details,* a magazine clearly targeted to adolescent boys. The article is entitled "The Pickup Artist" and offers advice on how to get a woman into bed:

> You met her and spilled your guts. She said you're kind of cute; she's never had a guy that's come all-out like that. Now, let's close on her. You want to get her into bed—that night. What you got to do is make her understand that passion sometimes is equivalent to love. . . .
>
> So it [sex] happens. And everything changes. Usually when we cross the threshold of sex, the woman falls in love and the man falls out. There's an old saying: A woman wants a man to satisfy her one and every need, and a man wants every woman to satisfy his one need. . . . You got to make a woman understand that no matter how compatible you are, if the sex thing is ill, it's not going to hold it together.[6]

Whenever I read this excerpt before a group of men, I see eyes begin to narrow to slits. I see nostrils begin to flare.

Wait a second, one man realizes, *that's my son he's advising.*

Who cares about your son, thinks another, *that's my* daughter *he's seducing.*

You got it.

When Malachi 4:6 (NIV) talks of turning the hearts of the fathers to the children, we know that this "turning" must occur because the hearts of the fathers are elsewhere: turned toward their careers, their hobbies, themselves. But the verse goes on to mention turning the hearts of the children to their fathers. The children, too, are wooed away from their fathers by a thousand competing voices. Fathers are aware of this competition for the attention and affection of their children. In our survey, they ranked this competition as the fourth greatest barrier they face in being an effective dad.

If men won't father their children, then there are others who will: rap singers, television, the school system, other kids. And we've got no guarantee that these influences share the same values we wish to give our kids. Often, they do not.

The media (television, music, movies, etc.) is one of your husband's greatest competitors. In fact, media is designed to be effective in winning a person's attention. Even that short thirty-second commercial on TV has a multimillion-dollar budget meant to guarantee that your child's attention is grabbed in the first second and not released until the last. That "old man" sitting next to your child on the couch is suddenly not as important as Paula Abdul singing the virtues of Diet Coke.

In the war for your child's attention, media may have won. Remember the study quoted earlier. Parents have dropped to third place in terms of their influence on their children. Media, which wasn't even in the top five a generation ago, has replaced church as an influence and moved ahead of the parents. Bob Pittman, the creator of MTV, the music-video channel, is so bold as to say, "At MTV, we don't *shoot* for the 14-year olds; we *own* them."

Busy, Busy Children

Other competitors are less conspiratorial and insidious than MTV and Ice-T. While some competitors seek your child's soul, other competitors are simply content with his time. It is very possible that your children are even busier than your husband. It may be *they* who don't have the time to spend with him.

Soccer. Gymnastics. Ballet. Youth group. Boy Scouts. Brownies. Track team. Debate. 4-H. Paper route. Friends.

Sometimes I wonder if there are other reasons than safety to explain why driver's licenses aren't issued until age sixteen. (After all, if an eight-year-old can zoom down LeMans Motor Speedway on a Nintendo game, he can probably make it to the mall and back.) Sometimes I suspect kids aren't allowed to drive because otherwise we parents would never get to use the car!

These extracurricular activities are good for our children, and our kids seem to enjoy them. But even too much of a good thing can be bad, especially when they crowd out what is really important: a father and a child spending time together. I've heard of a number of fathers who have announced, "This Father's Day, and I don't want you guys to buy me anything. I just want you to stay at home and we'll all spend some time together."

You can encourage your husband in the competition for his children's hearts by doing your part in governing your children's schedule. It is good that children are active, and that they explore a wide range of things, but they don't have to do *everything* (even if "Janet's mom lets her"). You may also want to keep your eyes open for activities that the whole family can do and enjoy together. That way father and child can be together, even if they are racing through a busy schedule.

Is fathering more complex in the 1990s? I suspect in some ways every generation makes that lament. But we are wise not to ignore the obstacles that the world places in the paths of fathers. To know that they exist is one of the first steps in scaling them.

The obstacles described in this chapter are your husband's responsibility to face and overcome. The obstacles described in the next chapter, however, are things wives often place before their husbands. We asked men, "In what ways has your wife hindered you as a father?" The next chapter contains their answers.

Questions for Personal Reflection

Think about these before discussion group.

1. What is the greatest obstacle your husband faces in fathering?

2. What can you do specifically to minimize the obstacles between your husband and his children?

Questions for Discussion

To discuss with a small group

1. What obstacles have you noticed that prevent men from being better fathers? What has been their effect?

2. How does your husband effectively balance his work and family time? Can you think of any ways you can encourage him in this?

7 Ways a Wife Can Hinder a Father

Therefore let us stop passing judgment on one another. Instead, make up your mind not to put any stumbling block or obstacle in your brother's way" (Romans 14:13, NIV).

Kathy and Robert have four children all below fourteen years of age, and they live in a middle-class home. Robert is a young professional and Kathy spends her days at home, coordinating the activities of this growing family.

One day when Robert strode in the door for lunch, heavy tension buzzed in the household. Instead of giving Robert her usual greeting and kiss, Kathy was shouting orders for all of them, Robert included. As she passed him on her way out of the kitchen, she called back over her shoulder, "He's your son and you'd better get this situation resolved."

Robert stood there for a moment, stunned. Then he noticed David, his eight-year-old, at the table, leaning his head against his palm. Robert remained calm as he listened to the boy tearfully describe how hard it was to remember about leaving his bicycle in the driveway. It was his habit to dismount his bike while it was still moving and then leave it there as he hurried into the house. Robert remembered when he'd been eight, and almost grinned. Yet he knew something had to be done, because by this time David's carelessness had become habitual despite frequent warnings. He assumed his calm, firm, disciplinary tone of voice and sent David to his room.

That's when Kathy stormed back into the kitchen. She'd been listening to the entire conversation, and this wasn't at all what she had in mind. "Robert, you've got this whole situation out of perspective. David needs a spanking and he needs to be grounded."

The other kids looked on with trepidation as Robert stood there, considering what he should do next. Should he go against his wife or follow through on her demand? She had strong ideas about what needed to be done, and she expected prompt action on Robert's part. Robert did end up going in to discipline David, but he did not ground the boy.

It was that evening, when David came down for dinner, that Kathy brought up the situation again. "David," she said, "you deserved the spanking, and you deserve much more. You're grounded for the next week."

Maybe Kathy had grown up in a home without a father, where she learned that fathers cannot be counted on, and mothers know what's best for their children and have to make sure discipline is carried out. Because of her low opinion of fathers, she has become a hindrance for Robert instead of a teammate.

By overruling Robert in front of the entire family she did *not* do what's best for her children. She humiliated her husband, and effectively said that he is incompetent as a father. Such actions will discourage a man's participation not only in discipline but in many other aspects of parenting. What kind of father is Robert today? He travels to conventions as often as possible, and when he's home he tiptoes around the house, trying to stay out of his wife's way.

Letting a Father Father

I fear that similar incidents are happening every day, and I expect most wives agree that this situation is the opposite of what they want for their husbands and families. But it's possible to hinder a husband in his fathering in quieter, less drastic ways.

What each mother desperately needs is to learn to understand her husband and not discourage him in his desire to become involved with the family *in his way.* He needs to be allowed to define his own fathering first and then express it, instead of having his wife ordering him around, telling him what a father should be. Once he figures out what his role as a father is, your role is to help him reflect on that definition and expand it or refine it. But if you chase him around yelling and nagging, most often it will only cause him to run.

Nancy has a story that illustrates this quite well:

> There were a few times when I've felt that Judd was being too firm or unreasonable with the kids, but now I can see the benefits they've reaped from learning to respect their father's authority. Fortunately, on many occasions I've been stopped before I could short-circuit Judd's wisdom as he dealt with the kids.
>
> For example, this summer our daughter Sara passed a milestone: her first job. She worked at a fast-food restaurant that appeared to be understaffed, and at times she felt forced to work eight hours without a break.
>
> Her second evening on the job, Judd and I stopped in to see how Sara was doing (on the pretext of getting a banana split). Walking up to the counter, we saw what I recognized as her "determined" smile. She leaned across the counter and kept a pleasant face, but with a desperate urgency in her voice, she whispered, "I'm quitting!" We tried to smile encouragingly as we stepped back and waited for her to fill our order. I could see she was trying with all her strength to stay on task

and not burst out in tears as she threw out the order she had just made and was shown the "correct" way to get ice cream out of the machine. To her credit she never lost her cool, and never lost her sweet, if slightly trembling, smile.

Since she was working the late shift and didn't get home till after one o'clock, we waited until the next day to get the full report of her work day. With many tears, she begged to be able to quit. And this is where the mother in me could "see" the "need" and identify with it almost too closely. I didn't want my little girl to suffer. I suffered with her. It was hard for me to distance myself enough to see the situation from a long-range perspective.

So Judd and I talked. Judd, who to his credit also struggled with her pain, could distance himself enough to make a wise decision based on what would be best for Sara in the future. "She made a decision," he said, "and decisions involve commitment. I think if Sara perseveres in this, it'll be easier for her to persevere later on in a lot tougher situations."

I sat at the other end of the table, imagining how Sara would receive these words and remembering again in my mind my little girl struggling at the ice cream machine. In the end, though, it wasn't difficult to accept what Judd had to say, for three reasons. First, I saw the wisdom in encouraging our daughter to endure. But, second, I also realized that this was an opportunity to encourage my husband, to affirm him in his assessment of Sara and the situation. And third, I found the freedom to allow Judd to make the decisions he had to make as father because I focused on what I was able to contribute to the discussion. I didn't sit mutely by. I really believed that I knew how Sara felt, and I reflected Sara's feelings back to Judd and gave feedback in this area. "Judd, let's not forget how shy Sara is. I can imagine even approaching a customer and saying, 'May I help you?' is stressful enough, without the added pressure of the pace and a tough boss."

It was one occasion where I did my part and allowed Judd to do his. Together we made the decision that, although we would encourage and support her as much as possible, it would be in Sara's best interest to continue in her job, learning to give God thanks for the difficult times as well as the good and easy times. I think Sara benefited. And I benefited, too. I left our discussion feeling that Judd and I had worked well as a team.

What Men Say about Their Wives

This is the last chapter in our section on understanding your children's father. We could perhaps entitle this chapter, "How Husbands Perceive Their Wives." Yet the chapter would be incomplete if I didn't remind you of what fathers have already told us at the National Center: "Our wives are one of the most significant influences in our fathering." You have tremendous potential for influencing your husband for good. This chapter on the possible ways to hinder your husband merely lists how your influence can be used negatively. They are the things that you will want to put off so that you can put on the positive, encouraging efforts Nancy describes in the next section. If you purpose in your heart not to hinder your husband, it's amazing how much energy is released to do the positive, encouraging work that truly yields results.

In various samplings, we asked over 150 dads how their

wives have discouraged them as fathers. In particular, we asked three questions:

1. How has your wife discouraged you as a father?
2. What obstacles keep you and your wife from working as a team to help your children?
3. What word describes your feelings about your wife's influence on your relationship to your kids?

The responses to these questions were enlightening, and I'm giving you the opportunity to benefit from them.

To put this into perspective, I want to make it clear that almost 50 percent of those men surveyed reported that their wives never discouraged or hindered them in their fathering. Thank God that so many of you are doing your best to be supportive, encouraging, uplifting, and understanding. That's great! Even though there are no perfect mothers, I hope you find it encouraging to know that your work is not going unnoticed.

But what about the other 50 percent? What did those fathers list as obstacles? In what ways did they perceive their wives placing roadblocks in their paths, causing them to struggle as a father?

These men report that they get discouraged when:

1. they feel threatened or belittled,
2. they are argued with or pestered about their fathering,
3. they are expected to be perfect,
4. a decision they make is questioned or reversed,
5. their own fathers are put down.

One way to avoid discouraging your husband in the five ways just described is to focus on the corresponding ways to encourage him. For example, one way to avoid belittling your husband as a father (and this may not be easy) is to think of some way to honor him. One way to avoid pestering him is to concentrate on giving appropriate and positive feedback. One way to avoid illegitimately undermining his decisions is to give him space.

In other words, we can overcome the hindrances listed in this chapter by practicing the positive encouragements of the next chapters.

In some ways, the five hindrances are merely symptoms of a greater cause. For what reasons might you as a wife hinder your husband? What is the ground from which these hindrances spring?

The National Center's research indicates a pattern which can be summarized in three basic categories:

1. differences in perspective that you and your husband might have toward parenting and life,
2. negative attitudes you might have which undermine his role,
3. actions which directly interfere with his relationship to his children, also known as perfectionistic mothering.

Differences in Perspective

Other than trusting God for your salvation, getting married was probably your biggest step of faith. No matter how long your engagement stretched, no matter how much marital counseling you sought, when you finally stood there and said your vows, "for better or worse," there's no way you could have anticipated differences you have since experienced with your husband. I'm not just thinking about who leaves the toilet seat up or down, or where he squeezes the toothpaste. There are much bigger differences that start to surface when your children are born and begin to come of age. Fathers listed several differences which they perceived as obstacles to their fathering. One man mentioned differences in their "philosophies on discipline, household tasks for children, etc." Another man writes of "tensions between family and career and the values/meaning husband and wife assign to each."

When Pete and Rhonda married, there was a big chasm to be bridged in terms of their backgrounds. Pete grew up in an urban setting, while Rhonda came from a small rural community. He was an only child; she was the fourth of six. Pete's family had a considerable amount of disposable income, and Rhonda's family squeaked by from year to year. It became particularly clear that Rhonda was hindering Pete in his fathering when she expected him to father in the same way her father had. "My dad didn't do it this way," she would quickly retort to Pete, "and he raised six successful children." (At such times, Pete thought, *No, he only raised* five *successful children.*)

Rhonda's father was very quick to administer discipline and call the troops to order. With six children, he had to. But Pete was very laid back in his approach, careful not to wound or expect too much from the child. As the years have gone by, the sparks continue to fly between this couple. Pete struggles to be a good father, and confesses that at times he wants to give up under the weight of Rhonda's expectations.

There *are* ways to get out from under the weight of different perspectives and different expectations.

Appreciate the Broader Input Your Children Are Receiving
Perhaps there is more than one way to parent (or even
father) a child. If there were only one perfect way, then I suspect someone would have stumbled upon it long ago, and
parents could now be producing perfect children like cook-
ies from a cookie cutter.

It is no mistake that your children have the father they do.
God intended it. And God has prepared him in a million different ways to be the father he is at this moment. Oh, your
husband is still responsible for the mistakes he makes as a
dad, but the unique strengths he brings to the parenting
team are the strengths God intended, even if they do differ
from what you might have had in mind.

God intends to benefit your children through the combination of your strengths and your husband's strengths. As a
team, your responsibility is to work at making your differences *complementary* instead of *contradictory.* The first step
is in allowing the possibility that maybe other ways of fathering are not *bad,* but simply *different. Vive la différence!*

Consciously Practice Your Vow to "Leave and Cleave"
There is another vow that shows up in many weddings: "a
man will leave his father and mother and be united to his
wife, and they will become one flesh" (Genesis 2:24, NIV). We
commonly refer to it as the "leave and cleave" passage. A big
part of that leaving and cleaving is putting to rest any expectations you may have for your husband that are based upon
your own father, whether you are remembering a loving,
committed father or if you are reacting to the many things
your father did wrong. Marriage takes two people who are
different and, by joining them, creates something unlike
either one. As you trust God's design for marriage, the

result will be *better* because of the unique blend of attributes. When you place expectations on your husband, you inhibit the good things God has in store for your marriage and, ultimately, your children.

Communicate Expectations

Of course, communication begins with listening, not with talking. *Seek first to understand.* Differences in perspective you discuss beforehand don't need to become issues to argue over later on. Ask your husband why he does what he does. Ask him what he saw in his own father that he is trying to emulate. Make sure you ask these questions with the intention of hearing his answers and learning his perspective. Don't ask the questions simply as convenient lead-ins to presenting your own views.

If your husband doesn't wish to talk about such things, there are other ways to get his perspective. Talk to your own dad. Talk to other fathers about fathering. Obviously, they won't be able to give you your husband's unique perspective, but they can give you some of the general perceptions men have, and they can open your eyes to all the different ways men try to be effective fathers. And, of course, there are a number of books available on fathering, written from a male perspective.

Seek first to understand, and then you can seek to be understood. There is nothing wrong in telling your husband, "This is the concept I've inherited of what a father should be and do." It's best if you voice this before a crisis; in a crisis, he might perceive your viewpoint as criticism. Follow up your comments with the question, "In what ways do you think my perspective is and is not a good one?"

Negative Attitudes

There is a big difference between discernment and negative attitudes. Discernment means being able to tell the difference between right and wrong, and is a gift of the Holy Spirit. A negative attitude is a predisposition to see everything as wrong, and to judge people, not behavior. A negative attitude can be very harmful. Any negative attitudes that you have toward your husband, toward his fathering, or toward fatherhood in general may get expressed through belittling your husband, publicly questioning his decisions, or belittling his own father.

One father reported, "She always points out what I failed to do." (You can tell how emotional the situation has become by his use of the word *always*—I doubt his wife *always* points out his failures, but his perception is that her negative attitude *always* governs their interaction.) Another man writes of being discouraged when his wife "confronted my fathering in front of the kids. I probably needed to be corrected, but at a more appropriate time."

Perhaps this man sums up the issue well. Your husband may *not* be a particularly effective father. What he does may often deserve a negative label. But are there more appropriate ways to point this out? More importantly, are there more *effective* ways to point this out?

Fostering a negative attitude toward your husband's fathering—however much you might think a negative attitude is warranted—will only undermine what you want to do for the kids (and it will make your life miserable as well). A negative attitude will blind you to those things your husband does do well. You begin to block off your husband's interaction with your children and, in "saving" the kids from his weaknesses, you deny them his strengths, too. For your-

self, you block any possibility of working with your husband
as a team and preclude the potential intimacy that could be
one of your greatest rewards as a teammate. In addition, you
spend so much of your time and energy focused on what
your yokemate is doing wrong that you begin to neglect pulling your own load. The moment you start trying to be more
of the father, your kids lose part of their mother.

Of course, I think the greatest reason to fight off a negative attitude is that the expression of such an attitude never
works. More change is accomplished through a proactive
approach (which includes positive feedback) than by wallow-
ing in your negative emotions. According to perhaps the
world's worst-imaged proverb, "Honey attracts more flies
than vinegar."

If you identify a negative attitude on your part that often
expresses itself in hindrances to your husband's fathering,
consider adopting the two following suggestions:

1. Check to see If There Is a Broader Context to Your Negativism

Perhaps your negative attitude does not reflect your true
feelings toward your husband; perhaps they reflect deeper
feelings toward fatherhood in general or your own father in
particular.

During World War II, thousands of Japanese-Americans
on our West Coast were rounded up and shipped off to deten-
tion centers. As our government has now admitted, our negative attitude toward those Americans was not based on fact.
Most of those detainees were fine, productive, even patriotic
citizens. Our negative emotions were not ultimately directed
at them, but against the nation of Japan and the emperor
Hirohito; the detainees became the unfortunate scapegoats.
We made a tragic mistake.

You may have had a very negative experience with your father. Perhaps he abandoned you as a child. Perhaps he abused you. It is extremely easy to conjecture that all men are that way, that all men are like your father, including the one you married.

Perhaps your husband is, in essence, like your abusive father (even though he may have never raised a fist); but then again, perhaps he isn't like your dad. The only way you'll discover the freedom to find out is to work at healing your own past. The next chapter of this book will deal with that topic.

2. Focus on Keeping Yourself "Results-oriented"

Have you ever seen your husband stub his toe, and then proceed to kick the very thing that caused his pain in the first place? You may even laugh (quietly), and describe his behavior as "typically male." But what about women? Do they ever behave this way?

When your husband does something wrong, you have a choice. You can lash out with the negative attitude that washes over you. Your criticism or belittling may serve momentarily as a good release, but it does nothing to help the situation. In fact, it may even set things back, like trying to fix a TV by smashing the picture tube.

The other choice is to focus not on what was wrong, but on *what would have been right*. With this image in your mind, you can then ask yourself what steps you can take to make such an image come true. Negative comments almost never help. When you focus on the positive, you gain the clarity of mind to know which of the positive encouragements described in the next section will be most appropriate. Yes, you may have to confront your husband, but you'll be able to do it in a positive manner for a positive purpose, not simply to tear him down.

A critical comment or a sarcastic roll of the eyes could put a big roadblock in your husband's path and, depending on where he is as a father, could drag down his confidence with his kids. Criticism without a corresponding word of praise is hard to swallow. If you think your husband is not very effective, and in truth he may not be, you will generally go much further by encouraging him rather than nagging or scolding him until he responds. An attitude of disrespect and judgment of his role and performance may drive him further from his kids.

Perfectionistic Mothering

Is it possible to be too good a mother?

No.

Let me try a different tack: You stop being a good mother when you keep your husband from being a good father.

In the cultural icon of motherhood, mothers are a dedicated lot. You're as trustworthy, hardworking, and responsible as America, apple pie, and Chevrolet. (Though I admit I've never understood the connection between the three.)

I suspect being a good mother is important to you because your children are important to you. Unfortunately, it is easy for some to approach mothering with a perfectionistic attitude that demands perfection from everyone in the family.

"I'll get my daughter Alice dressed, and my wife will come in and completely change Alice's outfit," says a thirty-nine-year-old computer software designer (who we would normally assume is competent in most areas of life). "I find it annoying that my wife doesn't respect my idea of what's appropriate."[1]

Little Alice might not be *perfectly* dressed, but is she *sufficiently* dressed? Her orange shirt might clash with her purple overalls, but aren't there more important issues in life—like a father's involvement with his child?

James Levine comments: "When mothers don't appreciate a father's need to do something his own way, a vicious cycle can set in. Mother undoes her husband's contribution, he retreats, she feels unsupported, he feels left out, and both of them feel angry."[2]

Of course, one of the reasons why some mothers feel the need to interfere in their husbands' parenting is that they often *do* know the perfect way (or at least the best way) of doing things. Generally, mothers are more skilled at parenting than men. Yet if you as a mother also desire your husband's input into your children's lives, you'd do best to stifle immediate urges to jump in and correct situations, and instead ask yourself some important questions:

1. Is my husband's behavior really putting my child at risk?
2. Am I more concerned about what others will think than I am about my husband and child enjoying their relationship?
3. Will I short-circuit my husband from learning a new parenting skill by interrupting his problem solving?

Psychiatrist and pediatrician Mark Sands writes, "If a mother wants help in getting a child to sleep, it may not be best for her to instruct her husband to keep the child in the crib and pat him to sleep. The father may want to walk the baby. He wants to problem-solve too."[3] Granted, your husband's hands-on training involves your children. Sure, there are better subjects for experimental work. Nonetheless, children are more resilient than you may think. They will survive your husband's well-meaning blunders (just as they survived your own). What they will not survive is a father who has distanced himself because he cannot live up to his wife's meticulous standard.

In chapter 13, we will talk more about giving your husband space to be a father. The thing to confront here is a perfectionistic attitude, which causes you to perform your tasks well but at the expense of other good things. Let me invite you into the next chapter, where Nancy explores how to be healed from a painful past. Perhaps your perfectionism as a mother is a drive to do for your kids what your parents never did for you. Maybe you learned to never trust anyone but yourself. There's hope.

Statues of Liberating Love

One man in our survey described his wife as being "like the Statue of Liberty." What do you think he meant? Perhaps like a bronze statue anchored in New York harbor, she is emotionally sturdy for her family—a model of consistency from which he can draw strength. Perhaps like the freedom Lady Liberty represents, he finds freedom in his relationship with his wife to be who he is and give who he is to his children. Perhaps like a beacon with a torch, she lights the way for him to find satisfaction in being a dad. I can see many ways in which it is a nice image.

Men report that their wives are one of the most significant influences on their fathering. I am confident that there isn't one of you who truly wants to consciously tear down your husband and separate him from his children. But things happen, I know. Emotions flare up. Feelings get hurt, and love for our children can cause any of us to go to extremes. I hope this chapter has given you a little bit of insight, or has better equipped you to recognize some of the pitfalls into which wives can so quickly fall.

You can replace these hindrances with the positive actions that Nancy Swihart describes in Part 2.

Questions for Personal Reflection

Think about these before discussion group.

1. If your husband were to describe an experience in which you hindered him as a father, what would it be?

2. How has your husband stifled or hindered your mothering?

Questions for Discussion

To discuss with a small group

1. Have you observed another mother like Kathy who dictated to her husband how he should father? What was the effect?

2. How can perfectionistic mothering supplant a father?

Part Two

Encouraging Your Child's Father

by NANCY L. SWIHART

8 Deal with Your Own Past

In this section of the book, we will be looking at those practical things you and I can do as wives to encourage our husbands to be better dads. Being able to *do* something gives us a sense of accomplishment. We don't want to sit idly by, watching our husbands struggle for answers to this ever-changing, lifelong puzzle known as fatherhood. We want to be actively involved, supporting them with our insights, feedback, and encouragement. What can we *do*? we ask.

Yet at the same time, some of us feel overwhelmed. We feel we can't quite get a grip on our own lives, let alone help our husbands. We sense that the ability to encourage comes from someone who is strong and knowledgeable, someone who has it all together. And here we stand, wanting to help but unable to summon the strength or apply the knowledge we have gained.

Ken and I don't want to assume that all Christian wives are strong and knowledgeable and "have it all together." We know that many women have been wounded, whether by their fathers, by men who have abused them, or by their own low self-esteem. And it is extremely difficult for anyone who hurts from unresolved conflicts to walk in the yoke collar without limping or stumbling, or even giving up altogether.

There is always a certain amount that even a hurting partner can give to her spouse in the way of encouragement and insight. However, in order for a woman to operate at her highest, God-empowered potential, she must have dealt with the pain and the scars that come from her background. Only then can she put aside her own agenda, which is based on past experiences, and relate to her husband in the present in a free, godly relationship.

Past Pain, Present Problems

Do you have some deep hurts from the past which still haunt your relationship with your husband? Are you afraid to trust your children to his care, even though he is generally a committed and trustworthy man? If either of these questions strikes a chord with you, you are not alone. Many women struggle with the pains of the past, and those pains certainly carry over to the present.

For my friend Jean, it was a major issue when her husband Bob disciplined the children. She felt uncomfortable when he interacted with them, never trusting him to do the wise thing. "That's unfair, Bob," she'd say. "You know Bobbie didn't mean it." Or she would argue against the punishment: "Don't you think that's way too severe for the offense?" Firmly believing she was acting in the best interests of her children, Jean was always on guard for them, ready to step in and become their defender and protector. In doing so, she effectively controlled her husband's relationship with them.

Years later, after divorce and heartache, Jean is looking into her own patterns of relating to men. Through professional counseling she has discovered that she never processed her relationship with her own father.

For many hurting women, pain originates from an unreconciled relationship with a father. Bill Ewing, director of Black Hills Christian Life Ministries, comments: "I have never seen a female client whose struggles didn't in some way connect to deficits in the care she received from her father."[1] If a woman's relationship with her father was nonexistent or weak because of his absence or inability to support her emotionally, her involvement with her husband will reflect the fear and insecurity associated with abandonment. If she was sexually or emotionally abused by her father, she will have a very difficult time trusting her husband.

A woman who has had a healthy relationship with her father is fortunate indeed. I remember being at a church leaders' picnic one summer afternoon, where we played a "getting to know you" game. We were all asked the question, "What memory do you have of your home when you were little that made you feel warm and loved?" I vividly remember the answer one of the young mothers gave: She recalled sitting on her father's lap, cuddling with him and feeling very protected and loved. It was clear that she often thought of that moment, and it had influenced all her family relationships and her perspective on the world. What a lucky woman! What a blessing to have memories of her father that still provide a sense of security! Her father had given her an inheritance that would last much longer and go far beyond any monetary wealth that he could have (or may have) left her.

Suzanne Fields, in her book *Like Father, like Daughter,* writes: "Her father's imprint marks a woman's identity for all time—her sense of self, her work, her love relationships, her understanding of the sexual differences. . . . The important qualities of psychological development are strongly influenced by the first man in a woman's life."[2] Fields is familiar with Michael Lamb's research, which found that a child of a highly involved father will typically be "characterized by increased competence, increased empathy, less sex-stereotyped beliefs, and a more internal locus of control."[3]

If your relationship with your father was healthy, you are

fortunate, and your husband is fortunate. The two of you will probably find it comparatively easy to work together as a team. You will trust him, you will have confidence in his abilities, and your expectations of him will be positive and realistic.

However, if a woman has had a negligent, absent, or abusive father, her relationship with her husband has probably already been affected. She may assume all men are like her father, and tend to overprotect her children in an attempt to "protect" them from the kind of negative experiences she had. Or she may overindulge the children, wanting to give them what she never had. All of these reactions to her own father-relationship—the distrust, the anxiety, the domineering tendency—will only hinder the encouragement that she could otherwise offer her husband.

Many women have firsthand experience of neglect or abuse from their fathers, and there is nothing more difficult to overcome. The scars are deep, the emotions mixed and confusing.

Whenever I hear the hymn "The Old Rugged Cross," I am taken back in the long corridors of my memory to my bedtime ritual, the echo of my father's deep baritone singing in the comfortable darkness. As a three-year-old lying beside the great hulk of my father, I would sing along with his favorite old hymn. Looking at the ceiling, I could imagine that beloved old cross standing in the shadows of my room as I sensed the awe that my father seemed to experience.

In those very early years, I was "Daddy's girl." He was the rock that anchored my world. But then hard times came. My father was forty-eight when I was born, and his health lasted only a few years after that. He seldom had any energy for us children, and before long his marriage to Mom became shaky. Then the fights started. The angry words. The slamming door. The months of not knowing where my father was.

When he came back, no one mentioned the past incidents, and the root of the anger was never dealt with. So the problems inevitably cropped up again, and in time there were more fights, more angry words, and once again the sound of the slamming door. And every time the door slammed shut, "Daddy's little girl" was left again with the recurring waves of loneliness and rejection.

In my late teenage years I thought all males were unreliable, so I had a hard time developing any romantic relationships. Every time I felt myself drawing close to a young man, I would begin to construct barriers, trying to push him away before he left me. Yet at the same time I desperately longed for him to step across the barriers and be the unmovable "rock" that I had once seen in my father. A lot of healing had to take place in my life before I could trust a man enough to become my lifetime partner.

What I experienced before marriage was something many of us take into marriage: an absent or distant or abusive father who colors our entire relationship with our husbands. We may have donned our white gowns and left for the chapel, but we cannot truly enter marriage if we are still mired in the memories. Dealing with the past frees us to live in the present. Dealing with painful relationships with our fathers releases us to pursue loving, healthy relationships with our husbands. In fact, one of the greatest things we can do for our husbands is to become yokemates who are healed and strong.

Ken and I would like to offer three principles to keep in mind as you begin this healing process: first, do not look at your father without the presence of the Perfect Father; second, strive to look at your father from your position as an adult, not as a child; and third, realize that healing is a process.

Father-God: The Perfect Father

Ken tells the men at his seminars "once a father, always a father," meaning that even when the kids have grown up and left the house, a man does not stop being a dad; his duties simply change because his children have changed. They have grown into adults and the father must adapt.

In the same way, we can say "once a daughter, always a daughter." There is and always will be something inside us that longs for the perfect father.

I was fifteen, sitting in a sea of teenagers at a youth convention, when I "saw" that old rugged cross again, the same one that my father's strong baritone had sung about so many years before. And I felt as though I was immersed in the love that emanated from its beams. *I* was loved by a great God who gave his only Son. I was loved for who I was. I was loved with a love that would not let me go, that would never forsake me. No more slamming doors. I had never felt such security and peace. At last I had a Father who would never leave me, and I responded by grabbing hold of his love with the same trust that the little girl so many years ago had placed in her earthly father.

As I learned to be more dependent upon my Father-God, his love gradually began to replace my need for love and affirmation from my wounded father. The process of healing took a long time, but it always drew me deeper, deeper into the heart of my Perfect Father.

Your heavenly Father will restore the trust and faith of the little girl in you, the one who so badly needed a rock that would not shatter her, a father who would not leave her. He has assured, "Never will I leave you; never will I forsake you" (Hebrews 13:5, NIV). Because our Perfect Father has given us every reason to trust him, we can lay down our defenses. He has become the protector of our bodies and souls. Whereas your earthly father may have struck you, your heavenly Father through his Son chose to take the whippings and scorn himself—even to the point of crucifixion—rather than have you suffer the greater torments of hell.

And the love of the Perfect Father will begin to help you bridge the gaps in your relationships with male figures. As I grew to know Judd during our dating relationship, I recognized his steadfastness and trustworthiness. Yet as we drew nearer to making a lifetime commitment, I couldn't bring myself to take the plunge. How could I trust him completely through the years that loomed ahead? James 1:17 provided me with the courage to hand my life over to this loving yet fallible man: "Every good thing bestowed and every perfect gift is from above, coming down from the Father of lights, with whom there is no variation, or shifting shadow."

There *weren't* any absolute guarantees that Judd wouldn't desert me or be taken away somehow, but I could cling to the fact that my Father would never change his mind, never back out on his promises. God, my Father, my Rock, was giving Judd to me as a gift. Faith that God was behind our relationship allowed me to trust Judd.

The Perfect Father will bring wholeness to the inner person, healing the memories and the emotional bruises that have accumulated through the years. This healing will give you strength to become the kind of yokemate who can encourage and trust her husband.

When you begin your journey back to revisit your earthly father—and you must—do not go alone. Invite your Perfect Father to join you. He will reveal to you the attributes of a perfect father, and he will be that father to you. He will point out to you what was right and what was wrong in the world of your childhood. There will be times in your healing process when you will need comfort; God is a nurturant father. Do not look at your past father figure without the presence of your perfect one.

Seek Adult Objectivity

For some of you, the thought of forgiving your father may be extremely difficult. To forgive him may seem the same as accepting or condoning his behavior and opening yourself up to being hurt again. Leanne Payne, in her book *Crisis in Masculinity,* encourages the wounded person to forgive by coming out of the "subjective" position of the child into the "objective, safe, free position" from which you can "analyze, name, and accept the situation for what in truth it is and has been."[4]

The "subjective position" is you as the child, you as a victim. It's hard to gain perspective on a situation when every time you think about it you imagine yourself as that child again, helpless to stop what is happening to you. Consumed by your emotions, you sigh, "Look what happened to me."

But instead of seeing two people in the situation (you and your father), think of three people: your father, you as a child, and the adult you. The adult you can look back on what is happening between the other two people and analyze it for what is right and wrong, true and false, good and evil. In Payne's terms, such a position is *objective*: You see it from a distance. Such a position is *safe*: You can't get hurt as an observer, although you certainly can empathize. And such a position is *free*: You can look as long and as deeply as you care to. In this exercise, you can leave the feelings of the wounded child and move into the analytical adult, who sees the situation from a distance.

It is through prayer, as you invoke the healing presence of

Christ, that forgiveness will come. Confronting the darkness
in your own parents is extremely difficult. Yet, it is possible
to acknowledge your own part in the difficult relationship,
confess and repent, and move on to forgiveness.

Do not expect the parent to ask for forgiveness or to
repent and change. It is usually impossible for a needy person to give you the affirmation that you so badly need and
desire. Instead, ask God to help you accept your father as he
is, a person in need of your acceptance and love.

Payne recommends the following healing prayer, even in
cases when there has been no outward sign of remorse or
plea for forgiveness:

> Father, I thank You for creating my father in Your
> image. With all my heart I forgive him for not becom-
> ing all You created him to be. I realize now that he
> needed the healing that I am now receiving. Some way,
> somehow, Lord, as I accept and forgive my father, may
> his life as it has been handed on to me become all You
> ever intended it to be. Lord, I do forgive him all his
> offenses against me. I do accept him *as he is,* an
> unhealed and needy person. There but for Your grace, I
> would be. I thank You for all You made him to be, all
> You created him to be, and in Your name I will affirm it
> whenever I see it. I look to You now, for the affirmation
> I always wanted so badly from him. Love him when You
> can, Lord, through me.[5]

This prayer involves many steps in forgiveness (and may I
remind you that forgiveness is a process). First, you are con-
senting to the fact that your father was created in God's
image. You acknowledge the work of God in your father and

recognize the potential that is there. Many times this
"vision" can come only as you look through the eyes of the
Creator. But it can come!

Second, in saying this prayer you are recognizing your
father's need for healing. Instead of viewing him only as his
deeds express him, you can see beyond to the hurt and the
pain that caused the deeds, and his own need for healing.
This prayer helps to spark compassion for the wounds at the
core of his person, changing your image of him as only a
wounder. It enables you to begin to accept your father as he
is, a needy and unhealed person.

Another step in this prayer is recognizing and welcoming
the part of your father that has been handed on to you, the
child. Many times when we have been hurt by a parent, we
cringe at anything we see in ourselves that reminds us of
that parent. And so we reject the good with the bad. Instead,
we can accept and even welcome the part of our father that
has been given to us, and we can offer that part to God to be
used.

In this prayer there is also a willingness to affirm the
"real" person in the father, that part that still retains the
image of God. With God's help, you will be able to commit
yourself to affirming that real person when you recognize
him. This affirmation will be one of the most helpful actions
that you can take, and yet it's also one of the most difficult.

Payne gives this hopeful insight:

> Eventually God may give the grace to the child to reach
> out with a hand of blessing to the parent if and when
> the opportunity presents itself. In this way the son or
> daughter can begin to see himself as the "blesser," and
> is no longer to agonize over the fact that the parent is
> unable to bless him (or even reform) in return.[6]

Our fathers may never change. They may never ask for forgiveness. They may never give us the blessing that we yearn for. Yet, as we gain confidence in our healed relationships through our Perfect Father, we may come to the place where we can bless and minister to them.

Healing Is a Process

Regardless of how well we have adjusted to our past, there will be times when it will loom large and ugly in the middle of an otherwise beautiful day: the sudden, unexplained sense of abandonment, the irrepressible fear of being taken advantage of, the desperate need to "win" in an argument. When these times do come back to you, it can be easy to attach meaning to your husband's actions that goes beyond his intentions and the actual fact of the matter.

Several weeks ago, on a beautiful Saturday morning, I was standing at the kitchen sink finishing the breakfast dishes. I could hear the sounds of Judd's feet as he quickly scurried through the kitchen and wordlessly dashed out, letting the door slam behind him. Suddenly I was enveloped in a wave of irrational yet very real feelings. Once more I was a little girl, listening to the door close behind an angry father who was leaving *again* to find his separate way in the world.

And so once again the inner struggle began: *Wait a minute,* I reasoned to myself. *Judd is going out to do the things he loves to do. He needs to be outside after being caged in his office all week. He'll just be outside. I'll see him at lunch. . . .*

Right! was my whining reply. *He will hurry through his lunch and rush right back outside.*

Try as I might that morning, I could not talk myself out of those feelings of abandonment.

That "memory attack" discouraged me. I have worked hard at dealing with my feelings about my past, and most of

Maureen Rank has written a book I highly recommend, Dealing with the Dad of Your Past. *In the first part of the book, she deals with some cause-and-effect scenarios involving our fathers. Which ones can you identify with?*

If Your Father	Then You May Find Yourself:
... was absent from your home (or otherwise uninvolved in your life):	• less likely to trust in the love and security offered by any man
	• living with a vague, nameless anxiety that your husband may lose interest in you and leave
	• possessing few skills in loving or fighting or growing with your husband
	• dependently looking for your husband to be a father to you
	• settling for something less in your husband because "all men are no good"
	• idealizing your absent father, and projecting that superiority onto your husband
... did not express love or worth to you (through acceptance, praise and nonsexual touch):	• ironically (but tragically) marrying a similarly overbearing, compulsive, or abusive man (subconsciously believing that "this time I'll win his love")
	• marrying a passive man whom you can control
	• becoming a perfectionist, in an attempt to achieve your husband's love
	• having possibly also been wounded by a promiscuous past (to at least feel *some* man's arms around you)
... did not exercise godly discipline and provide sufficient guidelines for you:	• marrying a passive man whom you can control

If Your Father	Then You May Find Yourself:
	• or marrying an overbearing man (who will dominate you)
	• lacking a clear sense of orientation in the world
	• feeling insecure in the world and unable to benefit from your husband's protection
	• not fully aware of your femininity, since you had no maleness with which to contrast it
. . . clung to you and did not successfully "launch" you into adulthood or the outside world:	• running home to Daddy (in the same way your husband might "run home to Mommy" when you have an argument or problem)
	• annoyed that your husband falls short of your idealized expectations for a father

from Maureen Rank, Dealing with the Dad of Your Past *(Minneapolis, Minn.: Bethany House, 1990), pp. 22-56.*

the time I have felt that God has healed those memories and filled my emptiness with his own love and security. Yet, here I was, about to write a chapter on the healing of broken relationships with fathers, and my own relationship with my husband was still haunted by the very memories I thought I had left behind.

Once I recognized where these feelings were coming from, I realized they had nothing to do with Judd's actions, only the way I was interpreting them. I then was able to own the feelings, give them over to God and make practical plans for avoiding that desertion syndrome in the weeks to come.

A few weeks later, after I had dealt with my feelings, I

explained to Judd what I'd felt and why. The revelation surprised him. Yes, I had been rather grouchy and accusatory that day, but Judd had chalked it up to "just one of those days." It was helpful for both of us to recognize the source of the problem and make accommodations. Judd tried to move a little more slowly, be a little more perceptive of my moods, and spend a little more time over the lunch hour. And I planned my agenda for the day with Judd in mind, spending some time with him as he fixed the fences or moved the cattle.

Hebrews 11:1 is a verse I have always held dearly: "Now faith is the assurance of things hoped for, the conviction of things not seen." We will experience victories on this earth because our healing is promised through Christ. But just as one who, long after his hospital stay, bears scars left from surgery, most of us will carry the scars from a painful childhood. We live in a fallen world, and we will experience the effects of that fallen world until we are taken up into glory. Only there will our healing be complete. However, as we grow to love and understand our Father God, and live by the conviction that he lives in us and is in the process of perfecting us, we can hold on to the hope of the glory that is ahead.

Be encouraged! Victory over painful memories, over distorted images, over broken hearts is possible. God's healing hand will mend the brokenness. He will be the Father that we never had. And he will enable us to walk beside our husbands, healed, whole, and able to encourage our yokemates in their walk.

Further Help for Deep Pain

We all have different backgrounds. Each of you has a unique set of complicated issues that causes pain to bleed through your past into your present. Absent fathers inflict different scars than abusive fathers. A sexually abusive father adds a whole new tragic dimension to the damage that a verbally abusive father causes. Divorced fathers leave a different hurt than deceased fathers. Your particular path of healing may need more specific guidance than what this book can give.

If you struggle with issues from your past that hinder your effectiveness as a wife, Ken and I would like to suggest that you continue to seek God's healing until you have felt his total work in your life. You may consider reading some of the books we have referred to which are devoted to helping you find healing in your relationship with your father. Second, consider discussing these issues with a professional counselor. In his book *The 7 Secrets of Effective Fathers,* Ken describes periods of counseling as "mid-course corrections." Sometimes the best thing you can do for your husband and children and for yourself is to stop and say, "Help. I can't think this through on my own. These maps that my parents gave me on how to nurture and guide my family are wrong. I need to chart a new course, but I don't know how." Ask your pastor or a friend for a referral to a good Christian counselor.

Questions for Personal Reflection

Think about these before discussion group.

1. Spend some time trying to understand your father. Make a list of his positive qualities.

Find out as much as you can about his formative years.

Did he have pain in his life?

How did he handle the pain?

2. Write down the feelings that you have for your father, both positive and negative.

3. If there is pain, can you see beyond the pain to the need that is (or was) in your father's life? What is God showing you about your father's need?

4. If your relationship with your father still needs healing, spend time alone or with a friend in prayer for this relationship. Ask God to heal your past. Pray the prayer in this chapter slowly, with an open heart before God.

Questions for Discussion

To discuss with a small group

1. What are some good and positive memories that you have of your father?

2. What qualities do you see in your husband that are like your father?

3. What reactions do you have toward your husband that may stem from the old relationship that you had with your father?

How can you handle these?

4. Can you see positive ways your dad has influenced you? Do you see your dad sometimes in the things you do now, as an adult?

5. If you have experienced healing from your past, would you like to share your experiences to help encourage others who may be struggling?

9 Stand Tall in the Yoke

If you were ever to be given the task of judging a team of oxen pulling a load, you could be certain that the posture of the teammates would be an important part of the judging criteria. The posture of the animals pulling the load determines both their strength and their endurance.

So it is with yokefellows in marriage. Many times, because we lack God-centered inner strength, we lean toward our husbands, or toward friends and others, or we almost bend double to draw out of ourselves the strength and affirmation we need. When we focus on our husbands, on other mothers or friends, or on ourselves, we lose our balance and our direction. Rather than doing our job in obedience to Christ, we try to please our husbands, to fit into the mold of other mothers and women, or to fill ourselves with a false sense of self-esteem. As we lean away from the center, we weaken the team, and in these "positions of weakness" we lack the strength to pull our own load, let alone to encourage our husbands.

Positions of Weakness

Bent toward Our Husbands

From the time of my conversion at fifteen and onward, my faith sank deep roots into Christ. I learned first from his Word and then from experience what it was to be loved, to be led by his Spirit, to walk in daily fellowship with him. I

learned to treasure my relationship with God above any relationship on earth.

Before I was married I thought long and hard about the
proper and biblical approach I should take toward a husband. Because of some obvious failures I saw in my parents'
relationship, I wanted to know what God's Word had to say
about this very important and lifelong commitment that I
would make to another person. I grabbed hold of the current ideas among my Christian friends and pondered ser-
mons I heard on the role of wives, especially concerning
submission. Wanting to prove to the world that a biblical relationship was the best relationship, I'm afraid I focused more
on the *idea* of submission than on God's intention, and I carried this concept to its extreme.

Therefore, once I was married I found my loyalties torn.
The overriding principle I followed was "biblical submission" to my husband, so I busied myself with the children
and tried to do everything I could to make Judd happy, tried
to find my happiness in him. Judd was a wise and God-fearing man, so it was easy to leave the decision making up to
him. In the process, I gave up asking God directly for guidance and trusted my husband for that communication.

But something was wrong. I soon discovered that my goal
of making Judd happy all the time wasn't always successful,
nor was it quite as fulfilling as I had thought it would be. And
even though Judd would repeat time and time again, "Nancy,
it isn't your responsibility to make me happy," I was convinced that this was part of my "submissive wife" routine.
And to tell the truth, Judd was not filling all of my needs
either, nor was he assuming the responsibility!

Oh, our marriage was going along just fine; we were a
functioning and intact family, and our children were developing nicely. But I began to feel a deep sense of loss.

I clearly remember lying in bed one night after the house had settled down and the children and Judd quietly slept. As I lay there, a strong feeling of homesickness welled up inside me, and then the reason for the emptiness dawned on me. "I have lost God," I whispered in amazement. And I longed for the time when I felt my full identity in Christ, when I walked as the daughter in submission to my Father God and found my purpose in living for him. Without quite understanding how I had slipped into this predicament, I determined that night to discover how to develop a strong biblical relationship with my husband without forfeiting or shortchanging my relationship with God.

Many sincere wives find themselves in this dangerous position. We have been taught in certain Christian circles that we must be submissive to our husbands. And I firmly believe this, I must add. But for many who misinterpret the idea of submission, as I did, this means losing our connectedness to God. We let our husbands become the focus of our lives. They are the ones standing between God and us, interpreting God's direction and communication *for* us. In this situation, we find our identity in our role as their wives and the mothers to their children, our main responsibility to obey our husbands.

The flaw in this interpretation can devastate a woman's relationship to her Father God and block her attempts to find her identity in him. In contrast to the woman who stands tall with her eyes fixed on Jesus, the woman who follows the pattern of false submission will lean more and more toward her husband's side of the yoke, focusing on him and what he can give her, listening to his voice of direction. In this bent position, she will stumble badly because she has lost her full identity and her true freedom to be the person God created her to be.

Bent toward Others

Our neighbors have geese. Occasionally when I walk down the lane to their house, one goose will spot me and begin its raucous honking, to which all the others automatically add their cries. They each convince the others that I am indeed some kind of threat, and they follow me down the path, drowning out my efforts to reassure them.

As I continue on my way to my friend's house, trying to ignore the geese's incessant noise, sometimes I think of how people resemble the silly geese. One person raises a banner and suddenly the rest of us follow, not stopping to weigh the consequences or check out the source of leadership. From kindergarten through life, we are impressed and led by what others think. Kindergartners fret over the right kind of lunch box. Teenagers follow their peers through shopping malls, crack houses, and sexual sin. And we would be naive to think peer pressure ceases when we get our high-school diplomas.

It is good that many Christian women get together for mutual support, but even this can cause pressure to conform. In many groups, the current issues are: whether or not to work outside the home, what kinds of contraceptives are acceptable, and whether or not to home-school. What is the right thing to do? How do we make our decisions? Can we be comfortable being different, basing our decisions on what we, along with our husbands, have decided God is telling us to do? Or do we, like the geese, let the noise of others drown out the calming direction of the Good Shepherd?

Maybe it's our fear of rejection or a sense of inferiority that makes it so difficult to block out the voices we hear, to not be influenced by what others are thinking or doing. Craving acceptance from those around us, we become followers.

We are afraid to listen to our own consciences because we feel inferior, we know we don't have it all together, and we are afraid that others will suspect the truth. So we lean outward toward others, away from our true centers, and stumble after the crowd. This off-balance position weakens our team. It forces our yokemates either to counterbalance us to stay on the path or to allow the entire team to be pulled along in a misguided direction.

Bent Inward toward Ourselves

In the Garden, the serpent told Eve that if she ate of the fruit, she would "not surely die. . . . For God knows that when you eat of it your eyes will be opened, and you will be like God, knowing good and evil" (Genesis 3:4-5, NIV). This lie from Satan continues to be promoted by many self-help groups and popular movements. If we lack direction and self-worth, they tell us, the answer is to center on the "inner self," the god within us. But this leads us to become our own gods, limiting us to what we think is best.

Recently Sara shared the frustration she felt after attending a leadership conference for high-school students. For two days the students listened to speakers who "encouraged" them with such statements as "You can be anything you want to be," and "It's all up to you and your dreams; whatever you dream, you can achieve." Nowhere, Sara said, did anyone say anything about looking to God for strength and direction. In their view, apparently, our destiny lies solely in our own hands.

This thinking directs us away from the strength that comes from our Creator God and creates a condition that is both sinful and incomplete. To look to ourselves for strength is to look to the fallen self, to listen to the creature that

"dwells in misconceived feelings and attitudes, those that
arise from listening to the self-in-separation and to the voices
of a fallen world."[1] We have been created with great potential, this is true. However, we can reach our true potential
only when we reach Godward rather than inward.

The Upright Position of Strength

What then is the position of strength for a wife who wishes
to encourage her husband?

The position of strength for oxen in the yoke is upright,
facing straight ahead, working together. We can do this with
our mates only as we draw strength from the Savior who
leads us forward.

It is the creature dwelling within the presence of its Creator who can live with arms stretched upward, face lifted
upward for direction. As Christians, we all have the potential to walk in this upright, vertical position by the power of
the Holy Spirit. Switching analogies, we need to be like the
sunflowers that grace the Kansas landscape in the late summer. In the morning their massive heads of yellow petals
face east, but during the day they follow the sun, rotating
as it sweeps across the sky to the west. Just as the sun-
flower receives its nourishment and life by facing the sun,
so our spirits are nourished as we stand tall, lifting our
hearts and spirits to drink in the power of God's Spirit,
undistracted by the other, lesser glowing lights which try
to imitate his glory.

This may sound like a confusing concept, but it is the age-
old principle of walking in the Spirit, the actual presence of
God. We acknowledge his presence as a vital Person who
communes with us, directs our path, and gives us strength
for the journey.

Our world is so attuned to the material and the scientific

that, though we want to believe there is a spiritual world that operates within our world, it's hard to envision it. Yet God stands ready and willing to communicate with our spirits if we are willing to stop and listen. We as wives gain our strength as we walk in an upright position of dependence, in communication with God.

When our son Daniel was three years old, Judd's father and mother ("Opa" and "Oma" to Dan) came from Indiana to visit us in southern California. As we sat around the dining room table we were all so busy talking that we hadn't noticed the intent look on Dan's face as he pulled his chair up close to Opa and leaned forward, looking him squarely in the eyes.

As soon as there was a lull in the conversation, Dan spoke up. "Opa, you're getting old, aren't you?" he questioned.

Amused, Opa cocked his head and answered, "Well, Danny Boy, I guess I am getting old."

"And you're going to die soon, aren't you, Opa?" Dan continued.

We all laughed uncomfortably as Opa answered a little more hesitantly, "Well I hope not soon, Danny, but yes, I guess I will die sometime. . . ."

"Opa, are you hooked up?" Dan asked, looking behind Opa's back.

"Hooked up? What do you mean, hooked up?" Opa asked.

"You're going up to heaven, aren't you? Are you hooked up to God?"

I'm not sure how Dan's little three-year-old mind envisioned this "hookup," but his profound yet simple image still lingers in my mind. I ask myself, "Nancy, are you hooked up to God?" I think not only of the weighty eternal questions, but also being "hooked up" in the way an appliance is hooked up, drawing daily power from God to be the woman, wife, and mother he wants me to be.

How do we stop and listen to this God who wants to communicate with us, who will help us walk in the upright position of strength? We must love God above anyone else on earth, listen to him when he speaks to us and, beyond merely hearing his words, honor him enough to obey them.

Love God

Where do we hear that clear voice of love that calls to us above the voices of our husbands, our friends, our world? For me, it first happened at the foot of the cross, where I was overwhelmed with the reality of God's presence, his matchless love.

As we become more and more aware of who he is, this love for God will grow and put all other loves into proper perspective. After his resurrection, Jesus singled out Peter with this very piercing question, "Simon, son of John, do you love Me more than these?" (John 21:15). Three times he asked the same question (by now Peter must have been haunted by the number three), and the Bible says that it "grieved" Peter that Jesus did not seem satisfied with his answer.

This is the question Jesus also asks of each of us. God longs for his creatures to love him. The greatest commandment is to "love the Lord your God with all your heart and with all your soul and with all your mind" (Matthew 22:37, NIV). When we respond to God's great love with our love, we will be able to say, "Take me, God. I am at your disposal." And we will be able to stand tall and not bend outwardly toward our husbands or others, or inwardly toward ourselves as we seek affirmation and purpose.

Listen to Him

What comes to your mind when you hear the word *solitude?* Impossible? Frightening? A padded cell? Loneliness? A distant rock battered by the waves of the ocean?

Or do you visualize something positive? A candle glowing. A rocking chair. Peacefulness. A quiet retreat.

Solitude could be called the "spiritual discipline especially for mothers!"

There is a vast difference between loneliness and solitude. Richard Foster, in his book *Celebration of Discipline,* says, "Loneliness is an inner emptiness. Solitude is inner fulfillment."[2] Solitude is a discipline we need to practice if we want to hear God's voice above the noise of our present generation.

Dallas Willard, author of *The Spirit of the Disciplines,* defines solitude as when "we purposely abstain from interaction with other human beings, denying ourselves companionship and all that comes from our conscious interaction with others."[3] In solitude we go off by ourselves: no husband, no children, no friends, no music tapes. Only the Bible. Only God and us.

"It's impossible," we say. "Too many people depend on me. I can't possibly get away and leave them alone." But it is precisely because we're involved in so many important relationships that we need to get away and focus on our relationship with God.

Willard defines a spiritual discipline as an "exercise in godliness." Just as a gymnast exercises her body in preparation for a performance, so we can exercise our spirits to gain the strength we need to perform in ministry to our families. Willard writes, "A discipline for the spiritual life is, when the dust of history is blown away, nothing but an activity undertaken to bring us into more effective cooperation with Christ and his Kingdom."[4]

If solitude were easy to arrange or practice, it wouldn't be a discipline. But we need it nonetheless. I remember my own struggles. After I made a commitment to reestablish my own connectedness to God, I was convinced that in order to do this I needed to spend more time in quietness. *Right!* With three little ones who had convinced themselves that my first responsibility in life was to be a mother, always available with a hug and a smile, how was I to find this "solitude" I so badly needed?

Taking time early in the morning seemed to be best solution for me. I didn't want to wake Judd with an alarm by our bed, so I decided to ask God to wake me early every morning so I could spend some quiet time with him. God was faithful! At 5:30 I would begin to stir, and looking forward to the next hour of quietness I would head down the hallway, past the boys' room and out into the living room. The first few mornings Derrick heard my footsteps in the creaking hallway and got up, asking eagerly, "What are we going to do, Mommy?" I don't remember how we solved the "we" question, but I do remember some productive times of communing with God in those early morning hours!

I have been impressed with the story of Susanna Wesley, the mother of John and Charles Wesley, whose household was full of children. Having no other place to commune with God, she would sit in her rocking chair in the kitchen and pull her apron over her head. When her children saw her this way, they knew that Mother was not to be disturbed— she was talking to God. My children probably would have thought I had "lost it" for sure if I tried that, but somehow Susanna had trained her children to respect this time when she needed to be alone with her God.

It is important for children to know that their mother considers being alone with God an important part of her life. They can be taught to honor this time, whether it is a particular hour each day, a morning every month on a retreat to some secluded cabin, a spot in the park, or a designated place in your own home.

God won't force himself on us by outshouting the television, the kids, or our own frantic self talking. Instead, he has given us the Holy Spirit, the Comforter, as his Presence within us to teach us what we need to know: "But the Counselor, the Holy Spirit, whom the Father will send in my name, will teach you all things and will remind you of everything I have said to you" (John 14:26, NIV). We can learn the spiritual discipline of quieting ourselves before God and listening to that voice that has promised to lead us.

Enlist your husband in your attempt to find solitude. "Honey, I need some time alone to get in touch with God. Would you mind taking the kids by yourself for a few hours Saturday?" Enlist friends to baby-sit. Times of solitude require planning, but they are well worth the effort. They protect us as wives and mothers and give us the strength we need to stand tall in the yoke.

Honor and Obey

After moments of solitude, we will have a renewed perspective of what is on God's heart. We are reminded of why he has placed us in this world, and what he can accomplish through us when we are obedient.

We know that his "worldview" often contrasts sharply with the worldview of those around us. God designed the world to work on his principles, and often those principles are going to look strange to other people. We honor God by obeying him in the midst of this world, by working for his purposes even though it *may* mean sacrificing the respect of others, giving up prosperity, or even facing persecution.

Let's look at prosperity as an example of contrasting perspectives. Our world tells us that the more we have, the happier we will be. We see it on television, and we even hear it in our Christian circles: "God has blessed me abundantly. He gave me a job where I earn twice as much as I used to." "God gave us the house of our dreams." I don't believe it's wrong to have material blessings, but when our happiness depends more on the *things* than the *God* who blessed us, we have missed the intention of his gifts.

God has called us to a life of eternal significance, and we know that material possessions will not last through eternity. (Given our recent experience with cars, I know they last *much* shorter than that!) God's command to "store up for yourselves treasures in heaven" (Matthew 6:20, NIV) makes no sense in our world's value system. But when we truly honor God, obedience becomes a rewarding part of our life-style.

God's principles also clash with the idea of upward mobility. Our generation naturally expects that the older you grow, the more you know and have and the more prestige you attain. After Jesus had questioned Peter's devotion and love for him, we read in John's Gospel that Jesus predicted where this love would take Peter. Jesus did not promise a bigger and better life-style, but rather *downward* mobility: "When you were younger you dressed yourself and went where you wanted; but when you are old you will stretch out your hands, and someone else will dress you and lead you where you do not want to go" (John 21:18, NIV). Instead of fame and power, following Jesus would mean a life of humility in communion with the heart of God, where there is true strength and power.

We women have a great investment in the success of our families. We care deeply about what happens to our children, yet often they fail, and sometimes they rebel. Our husbands may never be as involved as we want, they may never be effective spiritual leaders in the home. We may feel the increased heft of the yoke and skin our knees a bit.

But what will ultimately supply the energy to keep us going? Will it be our record of accomplishments? Will it be the praise of those around us? Or will it be the knowledge that we're pressing on toward a higher prize, with our faces and our spirits focused on Jesus, the author and finisher of our faith? Will he be the One to whom we look for our identity, our purpose, and our strength as we walk straight and tall before him?

It is through loving God, listening to his voice, and honoring his words that we are able to walk in the yoke with strength and purpose beside our husbands. Our true identity rests not in our husbands, our families, our friends, or even ourselves, but in our status as daughters of the Father through Christ.

Questions for Personal Reflection

Think about these before discussion group.

1. What are some of the big "issues" your Christian friends are wrestling with?

2. What attitude can you take in your decisions that will not put pressure on others to follow you?

3. Do you think that God's plan is for us all to look alike, or do you think he allows for variations? If so, in what areas?

Questions for Discussion

To discuss with a small group

1. Do you think that women have a natural tendency to look to their husbands for their strength and security?

2. Genesis 3:16 is sometimes interpreted that because of the Fall, a woman is bent toward her husband and tries to find her identity in him. Do you agree with this interpretation? Why or why not?

3. In what ways do we suffer when we try to find our identity in our husbands?

4. We have all felt insecure when we did things differently from our friends. Why? How can we know when to follow the crowd and when to make our own decisions?

5. What were you taught at home and in school about self-esteem? How can you fit this teaching in to a dependency upon God and his values?

6. Why is it so difficult to find our strength and direction from a spiritual being, rather than a living, breathing husband or friend? Has it always been difficult for people to deal with the spiritual world, or do you think our materialistic, scientific age has made it so? How do we overcome the difficulties?

10 Pray for Your Husband

By this stage of the book, you have been armed with "insider" knowledge about men in general. Ken has given you insights into the heart of your husband, and you've learned about the principles practiced by many successful fathers. You understand a little bit more about the obstacles your man faces in his fathering. And I have tried to help you see how your own father—as well as your relationship to your heavenly Father—influences your ideas about your husband's fathering.

So here you are, a concerned mother willing to do anything in your power for your children, and now you're ready to jump in with both feet to bring about the miracle of reforming your husband. You want to do something *now*. And when you think of *doing* something for your husband, you may be prone to envision particular acts you can do that will involve your hands, your feet, your verbal skills, your knowledge and expertise. To encourage your husband in his fathering, you may feel that you have to be on the alert—running interference, having an agenda, formulating plans, and arranging circumstances that will whip him into shape.

My first word of advice to is to lay aside all preconceived notions of how you will accomplish this miracle of making your husband into a great dad. I *will* give several practical suggestions on how to encourage your husband, but for now I offer a different, ultimately more effective approach.

Wellington Boone, an African-American pastor in Richmond, Virginia, has a strong vision for strengthening African-American men. Perhaps no other sector of society has suffered more from fatherlessness. People come to Pastor Boone and ask him what they can do to improve the situation of inner-city fathers. "I don't know," he replies. *"Are you praying for them?"*

The power to change lives for eternity will not come from our own talents and strengths, the things we say, the many deeds we do for our husbands and children, nor from the wonderful "how to" books we read. When our families are finally tried and tested in that last judgment day, we will find that anything great that we accomplished came from the power that streams down through our lifeline to heaven—prayer.

Our own efforts will be but ashes. Through prayer we are "hooked up" to the wisdom of God that goes far beyond our own human understanding, to the power of God that can bring down strongholds, and to the protection of God from weaknesses that can cripple our husbands and children.

In this chapter we *will* be talking about expending energy for our husbands, but that energy will be spent in time on our knees, in the quiet prayers that we offer on their behalf. As you grow in your practice of intercessory prayer, you will begin to discover that prayer is not just another demanding project you have taken on. It will become a way of life, as natural as breathing in and out.

The Way to Lasting Change

When I was a dreamy, romantic teenager, my favorite novel was *Wuthering Heights*. Catherine and Heathcliff experienced what I hoped to have with my own sweetheart someday. When she cried, "Heathcliff is me!" my heart sang out, *Yes, this is what true love is! When I find my true love I will*

Praying through the I-CANs

Let's not forget that the more actively we seek the specifics of what God wants to do for our husbands, the more vital and effective our prayers become. We can pray, "Oh Lord, show my husband how to be an I-CAN dad." Or we can take it one step further and identify the specific issues of involvement, consistency, awareness, and nurturance we see developing as your husband interacts with each of his children. Perhaps we could even chart it out like so:

Specific issues where I believe God is at work in my husband's life in the areas of:

	Involvement	Consistency	Awareness	Nurturance
Derrick				
Daniel				
Sara				

Children's Names

The boxes in the chart can be filled in by you with specific requests for the specific issues your husband faces in interacting with each of the kids. For instance, under awareness, I might pray, "Lord, please give Judd insight into what Dan is experiencing now that Dan is engaged to be married. Please give Judd wisdom in how to counsel Dan through his hopes and anxieties." Under nurturance, I might pray, "Lord, please give Judd wisdom in how to relate to his growing daughter. She is blossoming into a woman, and I sense that makes Judd uncomfortable in hugging and cuddling her."

You can review chapter 5 to refresh your memory about the I-CANs.

become so much a part of him that I will have his mind, I will understand his every thought; we will be truly one*!*

Imagine my surprise when, after I got married, I didn't become Judd, and he didn't become me! Instead of being constantly reminded of how much we were alike, I constantly bumped into the fact that we were very different. No mental telepathy here! I couldn't think good thoughts and pass them along to Judd, nor could he impart his wisdom to me.

Years later, I remember sitting in a family life conference at a large church, listening to author J. Allan Petersen speak on the importance of intimacy in marriage. "Your fingerprints should be all over the soul of your spouse," he urged. I liked that analogy. And I sought to make it a part of our marriage. Yet, we weren't Catherine and Heathcliff. Sometimes I learned things about Judd, but sometimes I was totally baffled by his actions. Other times he drew away from my probing fingers.

Once again, in God's great wise way, he reminded me that I *am* one with someone . . . God himself. Maybe all of my thoughts shouldn't be Judd's; perhaps I should seek to have the mind of Christ.

Through intercessory prayer we have access to a source who *does* know the hearts and minds of our husbands—intimately—yet with him there is no hint of the manipulation or control that can enter into our own very best intentions. And because only God knows our husbands' true needs, he is the only one qualified to change our husbands. God's spirit runs deep, able to wash completely through the hidden recesses of a man's thoughts and emotions, desires and fears.

Intercessory prayer releases us from the responsibility of having to know all the answers, having to be responsible for the actions or the neglect of our children's father. If we wish to be change agents in our husbands' lives, if we want to be catalysts for them to become better dads, then the only legitimate way is to join God's team. He is the one at work in our husbands as the master craftsman. He will gladly use us as tools made available to his skillful hands. But tools are all that we are. What a relief! What a privilege!

How then can we make intercessory prayer part of our daily lives in a way that will bring God's power into our husbands' fathering?

What Intercessory Prayer Is Not

First of all, I want to stress that intercessory prayer is *not* manipulation. "I know what is best for my husband. I know what he needs, and I will convince God to change my husband's heart."

Mary and Josh, a Christian couple with three young children, were committed to each other and to their faith. After some difficult financial setbacks, Josh decided to quit his job and move to another community where he could begin all over again. Because of the pressure he was under, he became very defensive and refused to discuss the issue with Mary. "Mary, I have carefully weighed all my options, and I have come to a conclusion," he told her whenever she brought up the subject. Josh refused to even pray with Mary about God's leading. What was she to do? Convinced that Josh was basing his decision on fear and not faith, she was sure their family was headed for disaster in this move. Would God abandon them because of Josh's headstrong decision?

So Mary prayed; but instead of praying that Josh would be *wise,* she prayed that he would *"wise-up."* She was convinced that the move was wrong, and so she asked God to block Josh from finding a new job, from selling the house, and from continuing his pursuit.

Intercessory prayer is not to be used to gather supernatural help on our side in order to move immovable objects (our husbands) in the direction we wish them to go. It is true that through prayer we have access to power that is far beyond our own. But to attempt to use that power for our own benefit or for our own agenda is to misuse and misunderstand God's intentions when he makes himself available to us on such a personal level.

Josh had refused to pray with Mary because he feared that her "prayers" were for his ears more than God's, that she was trying to manipulate him into a decision she wanted him to make. And he was right.

I recall listening as a child to some "intercessory" prayers going on behind the thin walls in our old apartment house. Our family lived in the front apartment, and we shared a common wall with an older couple. When our favorite cousins came to visit, we would lie in bed telling jokes back and forth in the darkness and then laughing hysterically. It didn't take much to set us into uncontrollable fits.

After a little while, we'd hear a voice through the wall. Unfortunately for her, Old Mrs. Z's bed was directly on the opposite side of the wall. She must have been kneeling next to her bed. "Oh, dear Lord," she wailed in her best fire and brimstone voice, "please, please send down a lightning bolt and strike those malicious children dead. Please get rid of them so I can get some sleep."

Poor Mrs. Z's petitions continued for some time while we lay there in the dark, fearing this somewhat peculiar adult and wondering whether God would turn out to be on her side or ours.

I seriously doubt that God will honor that kind of approach to prayer. When we intercede for our husbands, it should be with one desire: to get close to the heart of God and to seek *his* will for our husbands' lives.

Pray for Wisdom for Your Husband

Even before you picked up this book, you probably sensed
that there had to be more to a father's job than the obvious
tasks of protection, provision, and discipline. From the
added support of research, we can now confidently say,
"Yes, there is more to fathering. My husband is also trying
to be an involved, consistent, aware, and nurturing dad.
What can I do to help him?"

In later chapters we will show you ways that you can
model, reflect, and encourage these four attributes, but your
first major role is to pray for your husband.

Fathering can be complex. Our husbands may be wondering: What is the best way to teach my children and guide
them through the mine fields of their lives? Who are these
young people? What are their unique gifts and talents, and
how do I bring them to the surface? Fathers need God's wisdom as they go about the work of fathering.

And God has promised to give wisdom. In a miraculous
way, through his Spirit he has promised to enter into our
very thought processes. "If any of you lacks wisdom, he
should ask God, who gives generously to all without finding
fault, and it will be given to him. But when he asks, he must
believe and not doubt" (James 1:5-6, NIV).

In intercessory prayer we can be like the paralytic's
friends, who were instruments of healing. Through our faithful prayers, we can carry our husbands to the feet of Jesus
and there plead for the wisdom that they so desperately
need. "For the Lord gives wisdom, and from his mouth
come knowledge and understanding" (Proverbs 2:6, NIV).

As Ken has pointed out, many of our husbands lack role
models in the areas of involvement, consistency, awareness,
and nurturance. They will need God's wisdom as they

Praying against Fathering Obstacles and Pains

In praying through the fathering obstacles, your request is for God's power; in praying through the pains of fathering, your request is for God's grace. Here are some examples of how you might pray.

A Prayer for God's Grace in Overcoming Anger:
"Heavenly Father, you are at work to heal my husband's past and to give him a future of Christlikenss. Please heal him. Please conform him to the image of your Son. And in the present, O Lord, watch over his anger. Keep him from getting frustrated at his own weaknesses, and expressing that frustration in anger toward the children. Protect him and his children from sin."

A Prayer for God's Grace
in Overcoming Embarrassment:
"Heavenly Father, our children will fail at times. May my husband trust you, O Lord, and look to you for his sense of worth. When our kids do fail, please give him the grace to accept them, comfort them, encourage them."

A Prayer for God's Grace in
Overcoming a Sense of Being Left Out:
"Heavenly Father, may my husband receive from me and our children such a deep sense of honor that he is convinced he is an important part of this family. Show him all the ways you desire to use him in his children's lives. Help him develop his own relationship with the kids, without using me as the mediator."

---

endeavor to understand exactly what they need to do and how to go about doing it.

As you watch your husband fumbling around trying to relate to your children, whisper a prayer for him. Late at night as you lie beside him in bed and reflect on the awkward effort he made in his "date" with his daughter, pray for him. Pray that God will infuse him with wisdom as he seeks to become more involved in the lives of his children.

Or perhaps your husband hasn't reached the point yet where he sees the need to be involved. As he hurries out the door in the morning without saying good-bye, when he calls to say "something important" has come up at the office, you may long to scream, "BUT . . . your kids are here and they need you; they are important, too." At such times your heart can silently cry out, "God, please give him wisdom in ordering his life."

And, oh, how excellent it is to know that the cries of our hearts do not disappear into empty space. They fly directly to the heart of God, One who intimately knows the hearts of our husbands and who can communicate to them in ways we cannot conceive. Assured of this, we can wait expectantly to see what God will do.

Men also grapple with many questions as they try to live consistently and interact predictably with their children. How can I consistently portray my beliefs and values? How can I be consistent in interacting with my children? When does consistency become too rigid and inflexible? How can I be consistent when I have one child who is sensitive and compliant, and one who is in constant need of boundaries and consequences?

If your husband openly admits his frustrations, pray with him and for him as he seeks God's wisdom. Perhaps he may not verbalize his discouragement, but you have observed his unpredictability, his chaotic life-style that seems to keep everyone off center. Pray for God's wisdom.

Likewise, in your husband's fathering work of awareness

and nurturing, listen for his spoken and unspoken cries for help, and carry him to the throne of God.

Let your prayers be in the "humility that comes from wisdom" (James 3:13, NIV). Pray for yourself and your husband, that you each might be filled with "the wisdom that comes from heaven [which] is first of all pure; then peace loving, considerate, submissive, full of mercy and good fruit, impartial and sincere" (James 3:17, NIV).

Pray for the Tearing Down of Strongholds

We have heard it over and over again from the media, from family experts, and from our religious leaders: "The American family is under attack." The natural question is, By whom? I appreciate the leaders who have the spiritual discernment to target the real enemy: Satan.

The National Center for Fathering was born when Ken Canfield asked God, "What is the most strategic thing I can do to help families?"

He believes God's answer was, "Motivate the fathers."

Satan, too, has been looking for the most strategic way to get to the family, the most effective thing his evil forces can do to sabotage homes. Your child's father may very well be one of his main targets.

When Ken asked, "What is the most strategic way to motivate fathers?" he believes God's reply was, "Encourage the wives." Thus this book was born. We hope to alert you and encourage you to pray for your husband.

As Paul tells us, God has infused our prayers with more power than Satan will ever possess: "The weapons we fight with are not the weapons of the world. On the contrary, they have divine power to demolish strongholds. We demolish arguments and every pretension that sets itself up against the knowledge of God, and we take captive every thought to make it obedient to Christ" (2 Corinthians 10:4-5, NIV).

Although I had heard this passage many times before, I will never forget my "aha" experience when I realized the mighty significance of this statement of Paul's. We were sitting in our barn, a group of fifty or sixty of us, on hay bales and rickety chairs. Don Mostrom was presenting some ideas from his soon-to-be-released book, *Intimacy with God.* He reminded us that although we are living in the flesh, our warfare is not with the flesh; our warfare is a spiritual one and the enemy is Satan, who through his craft and deceit has set up strongholds in our thought patterns. This idea struck me deeply, and brought about a revolution in my prayer life: Now I had a real enemy to focus on. God has promised to tear down the strongholds Satan sets up in minds and hearts. I had a powerful tool—prayer—to use in dismantling the wrong patterns I saw in my own life and in my loved ones' lives.

Each father faces the strongholds of Satan. If the obstacles in his path become an obsession, Satan has his stronghold. A man's career, his lack of resources, excessive competition—any or all of these can become his total focus, and he may lose sight of what is truly important. We need to pray that God will block Satan from using these to construct his strongholds.

Greg decided to go back to school and get his Ph.D. when his children were in their early teens. He felt inadequate in performing his job because all his colleagues had doctorates and he didn't. So he "set his face" to the task. He was, after all, doing it for his family. It would give them more security if his job was secure.

The pressures to perform in his classes and also in a full-time job took a toll on his family. His patience wore thin, sometimes disappeared altogether. He focused on what needed to be done and instantly responded with punishment and harsh words whenever he perceived any mistakes or imperfections in the children. "Everything has to keep running smoothly. You have to do what I say, when I say it!" he would exclaim. He allowed no margin for error, no room for discussion.

Satan had set up his stronghold. One idea obsessed Greg, one goal overrode all else in his relationship with his family.

But Greg's wife believed in the tearing down of strongholds. Greg was beyond reasoning; anything she said to him at that point was like talking to a programmed robot. So she prayed. She asked God to break through the tunnel-vision determination that had taken her husband captive. She waged spiritual warfare.

God honored her prayer. There was no miraculous and immediate turnabout (though I don't doubt God can work instantly), but many months when she simply had to hang on in faith that God was working even when she saw no immediate results.

Slowly Greg became loosened from his obsession. He began to see the great rewards of being involved in the lives of his kids, and slowly he reprioritized his life. Eventually the family was back to normal—only better than before.

Many husbands face great pressures to perform in their jobs, and Satan would like nothing better than to turn these obstacles into strongholds where he can paralyze every father's abilities to interact with the most important people in his life, his family.

It is helpful to remember that our true battle is not with our husbands. Our husbands are not our enemies; Satan is the enemy. You will find this a comfort as you continue to relate to your husband during the days, weeks, or months that it takes God to "tear down the strongholds." And since our enemy is in the spiritual realm, it only makes sense that we use a spiritual weapon to do combat—*prayer.*

Claim God's promises for your husband. Intercede for him. When the stronghold is too great for you to handle in prayer alone, enlist other prayer soldiers to help you in the battle.

Pray that He Overcomes His Weaknesses

Ken has already described the areas in which men feel strong; but he has also revealed to you where they are vulnerable. Men sometimes feel embarrassed by their children because their names are at stake. Men feel anger from time to time, and sometimes when they express it they devastate their children. Many times men feel left out, inept, unneeded and unwanted in the process of parenting. And often they *are* alone, isolated from a support group that could encourage and help them better learn how to father.

The information you've gleaned from this book could leave your husband vulnerable. It would be very easy to use your new knowledge as a weapon. You can play the "I Spy" game, accusing your husband every time you catch him in an act that reveals a particular weakness. But you can use your knowledge to make a prayer list for him. When you see him lose his temper, you can also pray with him or for him. When he shares his sense of ineptness, you can not only instruct him (to whatever extent he is willing to receive your instruction), but you can also pray for his confidence.

Each of your husband's weaknesses can be overcome through God's power. God has promised to show his strength in our weaknesses: "But he said to me, 'My grace is sufficient for you, for my power is made perfect in weakness.' Therefore I will boast all the more gladly about my weaknesses, so that Christ's power may rest on me" (2 Corinthians 12:9, NIV).

Enter often into the battle of prayer for your husband, and watch his weaknesses evolve into strengths.

The Prayer for a Lifetime

My own life prayer has become a prayer that I extend to my children and my husband concerning their lives: That they may "know Christ and the power of his resurrection and the fellowship of sharing in his sufferings, becoming like him in his death" (Philippians 3:10, NIV).

My prayer for Judd is first that Judd may *know* Christ, which will take a lifetime of actively seeking deeper and deeper knowledge of who he is.

To know the power of his resurrection is to know God's Spirit, through whom we are new creatures, allowing ourselves to be directed by the eternal connections within each of us. I show that I truly believe in this power by kneeling daily on behalf of my husband and my children.

To know the fellowship of his sufferings means that I stand aside and allow God to work in Judd's life, not shielding or protecting him from the sufferings that God allows to be placed in his path, that he may mature as he shares a portion of what Christ suffered.

And being conformed to his death may mean that I watch as Judd experiences the pain of dying to himself, to his own desires and the comforts that I would sometimes like to provide for him.

Intercessory prayer means that we wives and mothers bow before God as we hold up our loved ones. It is a means by which we cooperate with God: We seek his will in a situation, ask him to give wisdom to our husbands, ask him to show us how he intends to use us, and, ultimately, entrust our husbands into his loving hands.

Getting Specific in Our Prayers

A prayer plan for your husband might involve simply praying through the I-CANs, praying against his major fathering obstacles, and bringing to God your husband's fathering fears. Another way to outline this might be:

1. *Ask God for wisdom for your husband, that he might know why and how to become more:*

   a. *involved*

   b. *consistent*

   c. *aware*

   d. *nurturant*

2. *Ask God for courage and strength for your husband, that Satan might not establish strongholds in the areas of:*

   a. *a scarcity of resources (time, energy, money)*

   b. *the explosion of knowledge (lack of know-how)*

   c. *competition for the hearts of his children*

3. *Ask God for grace for your husband (and protection for your children) as your husband confronts his negative emotions of:*

   a. *anger*

   b. *feeling left out*

   c. *inadequacy*

   d. *being alone*

   e. *embarrassment*

Questions for Personal Reflection

Think about these before discussion group.

1. In what areas have you specifically prayed for your husband in the past week, month, year? A helpful exercise would be to list these areas, the specific prayers, and God's answer to them.

2. What can you do today that will initiate your new pilgrimage of intercessory prayer for your husband?

Questions for Discussion

To discuss with a small group

1. Do you pray with the expectation that God will become involved, that he will act? How do your prayers reflect this expectation?

2. How do you know when you are praying with the "mind of Christ" or when it is simply your own bias or wish to control?

3. Do you find prayer an easy exercise? How can you incorporate prayer into your daily life?

11 Provide a Shelter of Honor

Imagine a line that stretches out toward the future. This line is the distinctive call God has given to your family. Along the line is a tiny circle, your family, moving forward slowly and steadily toward its goal at the far end of the line. The goal is to perform the mission that only your family, with its uniqueness, can perform.

Your husband, as the force behind your family giving it direction and purpose, moves it along the line. As the family grows and expands, he tries to keep it moving in a straight line. You, as the mother, give identity to the circle. You create the space in which the family moves, giving it depth and breadth, providing shelter and nourishment and an aura of security and peace. In other words, as the father moves the circle, the mother expands the circle. As the father and mother work together, the family will eventually move and expand enough to encompass the goal at the other end of the line.

Of course this is just one way to understand the distinctives that fathers and mothers contribute to a family. It's a simplistic picture, yet it communicates for me how mothers and fathers express their unique roles in the family unit. When the two forces work together, wonderful results take place. The family will find that it can comfortably and joyfully fulfill its unique calling, and will experience all the benefits that God designed for families.

How do we encourage our husbands to provide strength
and direction in our families? There are many different
ways, but perhaps we can be most effective by creating a
comfortable circle within which they can work as a father.
Men need to feel honored as they do the work they are
called to do. Without it, our husbands suffer. We mothers
have gifts that equip us to play a key role in promoting that
sense of honor within the family.

I enjoy browsing in little craft shops and boutiques. A big
part of the enjoyment comes from the aroma of simmering
potpourri that wafts in the air as I open the door. As I stroll
through the store, the scent follows me, even to the remot-
est nooks and crannies, enveloping me.

I realize that the potpourri simmers for a purpose. By creating a pleasant environment for me, their customer, the
owners hope I will be more inclined to buy that lovely doily
or that delicate bouquet of dried flowers. This is not to say
that the owners are mercenary. I suspect they enjoy the
aroma of the potpourri as much as I do, and they genuinely
want to make sure I enjoy my visit.

Our behavior toward our husbands can permeate our
homes like simmering potpourri. Our husbands can walk
through the front door after a frustrating day at work and
smell it in the air the minute they cross the threshold:
honor! They can walk into the study where we too are sort-
ing out a busy day, but there's a scent that joins the breath of
our kiss: acceptance! Later that night, they climb into bed
next to us and nuzzle their faces in our hair. They close their
eyes for a moment and enjoy the unmistakable aroma: comfort!

A shelter of honor, acceptance, and comfort encourages
our husbands in a thousand ways to be better fathers, to be
committed to moving our circles forward. As you radiate

these qualities in your home, your husband may respond to the godly goals you model. I believe this is part of what the apostle Peter had in mind when he spoke of husbands being "won over without words by the behavior of their wives" (1 Peter 3:1, NIV).

Or possibly a man will look at his circle of honor, acceptance, and comfort and recognize what great pleasure he receives from it. He may then commit himself to his family because it has become valuable to him, and he begins to move it forward.

Or perhaps a man who has been nurtured in your environment of honor, acceptance, and comfort will suddenly discover that he does have the strength to be the leader in his home.

Remember the fathering fears of chapter 4? When a man feels inadequate, honor can give him confidence. If he feels angry and frustrated at his weaknesses, acceptance offers peace. When he feels all alone in his fathering, or wounded from his own father, comfort can bind those wounds and give him strength.

Although we are not ultimately responsible for the emotional health of our husbands, we can make sure that the environment in our homes and in our families encourages them to feel honored, accepted, and loved.

A Shelter of Honor and Respect

The steady hum of rush-hour traffic was an audible reminder of Dad's imminent arrival. The boys and I had been preparing the house and ourselves for the "homecoming." This was a daily ritual, the welcoming apex to a day filled with the normal activities, excitement, and turbulence associated with preschool sons.

The boys had come inside from their backyard adven-

tures, were washed, and were occasionally running into the
kitchen, begging a slice of carrot, getting a reassuring hug,
and making sure the world was still moving toward *the
moment.*

The familiar sound of a slowing engine and the distinct
crackle of tires turning into the driveway outside the kitchen
window alerted me to the arrival of the expected dad. As I
heard the car door slam, I called out, "Daddy's home." A
spontaneous eruption of joy sprang from the boys as they
ran to the door, shouting, "Daddy's home! Daddy's home!"

It was time for father and sons as the boys fought to be
the first to tell Dad all that happened that day. Judd, working
hard to give his undivided attention to his sons, sent a quick
glance my way. Our time would come later. This was designated "Daddy time."

Though this scene seems like it "happened only yester-
day," it is far removed from our present crowded schedules
(now there are occasional days when Judd beats me home
from work). But those memories recall moments of great
honor, when Judd was made to feel valuable and appreciated
in his home.

In his book *Love Is a Decision,* Gary Smalley discusses
honor in a chapter entitled, "The Foundation for All Healthy
Relationships." Smalley obviously honors honor! "Without a
doubt," he writes, "the concept of honor is the single most
important principle we know of for building healthy relationships. . . . The results of allowing 'honor' to reign can be dramatic and life-changing."

The Greek word for "honor" connotes something "heavy"
or "weighty." By contrast, the word for "dishonor" means
"mist" or "steam," something lightweight and insignificant.
Smalley comments: "When we honor particular people we're
saying in effect that who they are and what they say carries

great weight with us. They're extremely valuable in our eyes. Just the opposite is true when we dishonor them. In effect, by our verbal or nonverbal statements we're saying that their words or actions make them of little value or 'lightweights' in our eyes."[1]

Ken Canfield says, "A woman's greatest need from her husband is to be cherished; a man's greatest need from his wife is to be respected." The more I think about that, the more I can see that a woman being cherished and a man being respected are really two sides of the same coin: honor. I enjoy when I am being cherished by Judd, when he makes me feel that I am a precious and beautiful treasure. Judd has that same desire to be valued. I can also see how that "value" spills over into honor for his accomplishments and honor for his position as head of our home.

Men feel the need to be honored for what they accomplish. Sometimes your husband's victories might seem small (maybe he figured out a way to fix the hot water heater himself), but he still likes to be recognized.

A friend of mine lives in the country where every year her husband buys a few baby calves to raise on their property. He may bottle feed the youngest, but eventually they all go out to pasture until he sells them in the fall. It's just a hobby, since he has a job in town. It's not a very profitable hobby, however. After the fall sale, he sits at the coffee table with a calculator and subtracts the original cost, plus feed and other supplies, from the check he receives. More years than not, he looks up at his wife with a sheepish grin and announces, "Another tax deduction this year."

My friend would joke about her husband and his "losses," until one day her adult son told her, "Mom, I wouldn't talk about the cattle any more."

"Why not?" she asked.

"Because Dad's just doing it as a hobby, but when you point out the loss on the cattle, he feels like he failed."

"How do you know that?" she said.

Maybe it was just her son's male perspective. Regardless, my friend began to reexamine *her* perspective. She sought to understand how her husband viewed the cattle, and what victories he did obtain. For him, it was a victory just to raise these calves to market size, because there have been years when he lost some to pneumonia. It was a victory to have the fence strung tightly and the barn kept orderly. It was a pleasure to look out the window in the early summer evening and simply watch the cattle graze contentedly. Her husband accomplished a lot through his "hobby," and she began to tell him so.

This story illustrates an answer to a question you may be asking at this point: What if my husband is hard to honor? What if he does a lot that is downright *dis*honorable?

Dishonorable behavior is dealt with through confrontation and through forgiveness (the subjects of later chapters). Here, I am simply asking you to honor *whatever* you can honor. If your husband does anything that is *honor*able (and you may have to make a conscious effort to find it), then honor it.

If your husband has divorced you and abandoned the children by his absence, but he sends his child support payments faithfully every month, then tell him how much you respect his consistency with the payments. The checks may in no way make up for the loss you and your children have suffered, and your honoring his consistency in *this* area will not mean you condone the overall situation. Instead, you are simply recognizing that at least keeping his financial commitments is in itself an honorable thing to do.

Honor what you can. In fact, it's a proverb: "Do not withhold good from those who deserve it" (3:27, NIV), which we often translate, "Give credit where credit is due." For some of you, this may mean looking long and hard for something—anything!—to honor. You don't need to be dishonest, just observant. If you are committed to honoring your husband, God will give you the eyes to see.

If for a moment you could set your husband outside the picture (and you may have to set your father outside it, too), how would you answer the question: What value do you place on fatherhood? Are fathers important? Is their participation crucial to the well-being of the home?

How you answer those questions will determine a great deal about how effectively you honor your husband for his position as a father. "My home is my castle," the men used to say, and they'd puff out their chests and purr contentedly in the backs of their throats. Some people would call that supremacist, and certainly with some men it was. But perhaps other men were simply reveling that at least in their homes (as compared to their workplaces, usually) *they are important.* For once they get the chance to feel kingly. Why? Because they're the king! And you, of course, are the queen.

As a little girl, I used to imagine that my dad *was* the king. He worked out of town as a skilled laborer and would usually live at the work site during the week and then come home on weekends. The memory of his weekly arrivals is still imprinted in my mind. I'd imagine that our simple home was a palace and that the king had been off visiting his lands or conquering other domains. But soon he'd be coming home. The cry of "He's home," would ring out and, as my mom related to us years later, she watched the flash of little fat legs flying to the front door for the happy reunion.

We can tell our husbands that "being a father is important" as a means of saying, "Why aren't you a better one?" or we can communicate, "Being a father is important" as a means of saying, "I'm glad my children have one; you are an important part of this family." This is the second answer to the question: How do we honor a dishonorable father? We don't honor dishonor; instead, we respect the honorable profession of fatherhood to which our husbands are called.

If we don't honor our husbands, we not only miss out on a wonderful opportunity to encourage them as fathers, but we actually discourage their involvement with our children. If a man doesn't believe he can make a valuable contribution to parenting, why should he bother trying?

Let me offer three practical suggestions for ways to honor our husbands:

1. Encourage Your Kids to Honor Their Father

What I did for Judd on his arrivals home was the same thing my mom did for my dad: We both incited in the kids an honest anticipation for their father's arrival. It was a "big" (or weighty) event in the day to see their dad.

"Honor your father and your mother, so that you may live long in the land the Lord your God is giving you" (Exodus 20:12, NIV). Honor is a command given to children, but mothers can teach their children to obey this command through role modeling. Children *will* reflect the mother's attitude toward the father. By modeling a sense of honest anticipation at Dad's return from a day at work, a mother not only trains her children, but she also indirectly encourages the father by setting the stage for respectful behavior in her children. Daddy *is* special. When he reenters the home, his presence rounds out the family once again.

When the family is together, enforce the command to

"honor your father." Let the kids know that dishonor is off-limits in *your* home.

I heard a startling story illustrating how the phrasing of a rebuke made all the difference in the world. A family was around the supper table when one of the kids said something disrespectful to his mother. The father put his napkin down on the table and stood up: It was clear he was about to say something of great importance.

"No one," he told his son, "talks to *my wife* in that manner. Do you hear?"

The child heard.

What's memorable to me is that the man did not say, "Don't talk to *your mother* that way" (which I would think is the common phrasing). Instead, he specifically referred to her as "my wife." He conveyed to this child that whatever he might have thought about his mother, the father had very different thoughts about that same woman: She was his wife, someone of great value to him. In one sentence, this man both rebuked dishonor and modeled honor.

We could try the same. The next time your children start to say something dishonoring to their father, let them know: You honor the man, and they should too.

2. Watch Your Words—Before Your Husband and Especially Before Your Husband's Children

The apostle James said there was one thing he could never quite understand: the workings of the human tongue. "From the same mouth come both blessing and cursing. My brethren, these things ought not to be this way" (James 3:10).

No, they ought not be—but they are. Mark Twain once said, "I can live three weeks on just one good compliment." On the flip side, I still smart from memories of offensive comments people made years ago. Your words are your best instrument for conferring honor, but they are also your sharpest tools for dishonor. Watch your words.

But especially watch the words you use when you talk about your husband in the presence of your children.

For a boy named Jake, the list of phrases his mother burned into his childhood memory would look like this:

> "Your father is a fool."
> "Don't pay any attention to him, he doesn't know what he's talking about."
> "Can't he do anything right?"
> "Let's celebrate! Your dad is going to be away for a while."

Jake's father had a serious heart attack and had been reduced to part-time jobs whenever he could find one. The responsibility for the family's financial support fell on Jake's mother, and she resented it. But when she voiced that resentment, she stole from her husband the one thing he wanted most, the respect of his children. And she stole from her children the one thing they needed most: a respected father. Ironically, she also robbed herself of the gift of an encouraged husband who would have actively gotten involved in his family in other ways besides providing financially.

One fathering advocate tours the country with a seminar entitled, "How to Be a Hero to Your Kids." Men respond to the title. Kids themselves may even talk in these terms. In an essay contest sponsored by the National Center for Fathering, one teenager wrote: "Awhile ago my father had picked me up from school after a stressful day and said to me, 'Sandy, one day I'll be a big star.' I turned to him and said, 'You'll always be a star to me, Daddy!'"

3. Honor Your Husband's Decisions

In chapter 12, we will deal with the give-and-take of parental decision making. It can be difficult. Sometimes he's right; sometimes he's wrong. Sometimes *you're* right; sometimes you're wrong. When we add the issue of biblical submission, the already complex discussion takes a whole new slant.

For now though, realize this fact: When your husband makes a decision before the children and you contradict that decision, you may actually do more harm to your children than you would if you had enforced his wishes, however wrong you might think that decision is. Remember, there are ways to deal with dishonorable decisions—namely confrontation and forgiveness. You are not powerless. But heaping dishonor on your husband by undermining his decisions will only hurt the whole family.

Men are sensitive about the decisions they make. "Has your wife ever discouraged you as a father?" the National Center for Fathering asked. One man replied, "Not often, but occasionally I feel deflated when she does not support me." Another man was more emphatic: "Yes, in not backing up a decision I made but rather changing it." Still another man reported that his wife would "reverse a decision I made; counteract something said or done in discipline." In fact, the most common answer to the question of how wives discourage their husbands was: by not honoring their decisions.

One of the worst cases I've seen of this type of dishonor occurred between Fred's parents. His mother thought his father was too harsh, too strict, and too repressive—and perhaps he was. As Fred's father left for work each day, he gave his wife instructions for what was to be done or for discipline that was to be carried out while he was gone. I'm not urging fathers to take their "kingship" this far, but the way the mother refused to carry out the instructions and back up the discipline dishonored her husband.

"Okay," she told Fred and the other boys, "I'm going to let you off the hook because I don't agree with your dad. But don't tell him. It'll be our little secret, okay?"

If he grounded them, she would let them leave or watch TV, covering for them, going against the demands she thought were too strict. She became their protector, and together they formed a coalition of control.

Today, the relationship Fred and his brothers have with their dad is strained. As young adults, they struggle with alcoholism and rebellion against authority. Actions intended to be in the best interest of her children ended up crippling them in their adult lives.

We have several options for dealing with decisions which we disagree with; dishonor is not one of them.

The biblical command is simple: "honor *all* men" (1 Peter 2:17, italics mine). Do we believe the Lord knew what he was doing when he gave us that command? Do we believe he was aware of some of the dishonorable things we encounter in people, even in our husbands?

The Lord knows, and still he commands us to "honor all men." Ultimately, he knows that honor does not rest in performance or even position. He knows that honor can be shown to any person, because everyone is made in the image of an honorable God. It's a further part of James's perplexity: "With the tongue we praise our Lord and Father, and with it we curse men, who have been made in God's likeness" (James 3:9, NIV).

The Lord knows. He knows that a home filled with the fragrance of honor is an environment where honorable behavior is learned, rewarded, and eventually pursued. And throughout the process, our husbands gain the confidence and the desire to be better dads.

Questions for Personal Reflection

Think about these before discussion group.

1. Take a few minutes to reflect on the "aroma" that greets your husband when he comes home from work. What are the good scents that may welcome him? What are the unwelcome or distressing scents that might be avoided?

2. How do you encourage your children to honor their father? Make a list of what you are doing, and the things that you can do.

3. Do you watch your words in front of your children? What can you say that will show the children you honor your husband, even when sometimes you believe he is wrong?

4. Think of a decision that your husband has made recently that you are having a hard time with. How can you show honor in your reaction to this decision?

Questions for Discussion

To discuss with your husband and/or a small group

1. Was your father honored in your home when you were growing up? How did this look?

2. What do you see as good patterns of honor that you have observed that you would like to follow in your own home?

3. What patterns of dishonor have you observed that you would like to avoid?

4. What are some ways that you can encourage your husband in his own particular accomplishments?

5. How do you let your husband know that he is important? That you are glad that he is the father of your children?

12 Provide a Shelter of Acceptance and Comfort

When the kids were younger I used to glance out the window and watch them play "tag" with their friends. Someone was "it," and the others would scatter as he chased them around the rose bushes and across the patio. But there was always one place—usually the old walnut tree—that was identified as "home." The kids would run toward it, dodge out of reach of the person who was "it," touch the tree, and yell, "Safe!"

Home. Safety. Two words that should always be synonymous. When our husbands walk in the door after a day of being chased around by various demands and deadlines, they, too, should feel that they are "home safe."

Providing a Shelter of Acceptance

A shelter of acceptance is a place where your husband is accepted for who he is; a place that says, "You are safe in my presence." Our acceptance is based on our love for him and our understanding of him. It is not a bitter pill to swallow, a sense of resignation: "Well, I guess I'll just have to live with all his shortcomings."

Instead, accepting your husband is positive, and focuses on what you can do for him. It has less to do with what *you* are suffering than with what you can *keep him* from suffering.

For many husbands, the workplace is very stressful.

Demands for performance tax his creative and physical
energy. Someone is always out in front, producing more,
thinking bigger, gathering more support. When your husband comes home from this type of environment, he needs
to be praised, to be recognized as a husband, a father, and an
irreplaceable part of the family. He needs to be "home safe."

Wives can create this shelter of acceptance for their husbands. If the saying "knowledge is power" is true, then you
are the one person who holds the most power over your husband. No one understands your husband more intimately;
no one knows his weaknesses better than you do. When you
accept your husband, you reassure him that you are not
going to use that knowledge against him by ridiculing those
weaknesses. You are not going to use knowledge to your
own advantage. You are not going to destroy him by revealing his weaknesses to others.

Our husbands should be able to feel safe in our presence,
knowing that we are committed to their growth and sense of
well-being. We must use what we know about them to help
them feel safe and productive.

How does acceptance from his wife help a man become a
better father? As with honor, the benefit is in the environment it creates. Home is a pleasant place to be when a man
knows he is accepted there, and in such an environment he
will be more likely to value his family and invest himself in it.

Acceptance will allow a man the freedom to father, which
includes the freedom to make mistakes as a father. If you
remember from earlier chapters, one of the most paralyzing
fears for fathers is a sense of inadequacy. Some men are so
afraid of doing something wrong that they do nothing at all.
I knew a man who refused to hold his newborn baby for fear
he would "break" her. An atmosphere of acceptance gives a
father the freedom to be who he is—weaknesses and all.

He'll be willing to take risks and reach out to his children when he knows he's safe in your presence.

We can create a shelter of acceptance for our husbands in three specific ways.

Accept His Earning Power

In this area it's vital that we, as wives and mothers, hang onto biblical values ourselves. Our society bombards us with the idea that our wealth and material possessions reflect who we are. There's even a common term bandied about the financial community: net worth. "What's his net worth?" someone may ask, as though one's money and assets somehow determine a person's worth or value. A husband may ask himself, "How much am I worth? Obviously not as much as Joe is to his family. Look at how much Joe is able to give them."

If we feel the pressure to look good to the rest of the world, we put pressure on our husbands. It may be difficult to feel happy with clothes from discount stores when all of our friends are buying their clothes from the fancy stores at the mall, to be content driving a car with 100,000 miles on it when everyone else is driving a new minivan, or to live in a duplex where we don't have room to entertain friends. But to learn contentment is to gain a great skill in accepting our husbands.

In one of my freshman composition classes, I witnessed once again the pain that men experience when they feel that the financial support of their family is inadequate.

One of my students offered to read her essay to the class. As she read softly, her voice broke occasionally. Her paper described a family conference at which her parents shared with the children some pain they had been experiencing. The pain belonged largely to her father, who had fallen into

a deep depression from feeling he was a failure. He was
unable to provide the comforts he had always hoped to, and
as Lorrie prepared to leave for college, it looked like he
never would accomplish his dreams. Because of his depression, they had decided to use some of their dwindling
resources for professional counseling.

Lorrie read her own reaction to the news. "But Daddy,"
she had countered tearfully, "we have so much more than
money can buy. We have you, we have your love, we have
security."

How wise for a young lady! She tried to make her father
feel *accepted* by the family.

This kind of acceptance is crucial. The work world prizes
financial success, but every family member, including your
husband, needs to feel that there are no such measuring
sticks in the home. A dad needs to feel accepted and loved
even if the job he has doesn't make it possible for his family
to buy designer clothes, take expensive vacations, or live in
a prestigious housing area. The typical father already feels
the weighty responsibility of providing for his family; make
it your goal to accept him for who he is, not for what he
brings home every two weeks.

Learn to Accept His Idiosyncrasies

We all have our own little eccentricities. And we all want to
be accepted in spite of them. Our husbands also have their
own unique qualities that to us may seem "a little strange."
One man may be a bear when he wakes up in the morning
before his first cup of coffee. Another may "putter" around
the yard looking for a bush to trim, a rock to move, a plant to
water. Another may get irritated when he drives in heavy
traffic, tailgating and trying to push the driver in front of him

along. One husband may think he looks charming in a full beard, when it drives you to distraction. He may snore at night. He may lack "sensitivity." He may not like to talk much, or even worse, he may not listen very well. Maybe he never quite hits the hamper with his dirty shirts and socks. Little things. Yet how we handle them will set the stage for a myriad of other interactions in the home.

It's ironic that some of these idiosyncrasies may be the very same qualities we found so charming when we first met. But no more, thank you!

We may feel that it is our "right" to shape up this human being, so we nag, complain, and criticize. The alternative is to accept. Acceptance does not mean that we don't confront if we feel that the behavior is dangerous (tailgating at sixty-five miles an hour, for instance), or if it is modeling unhealthy habits. When we do confront, we should do it in a manner that gives information, without demands, and assumes both parties want what is best. We express concerns positively and sincerely, and then—what is especially important for us to learn—we let go. We give his idiosyncrasies over to God, and then we are free to love and accept him despite the little irritations.

How will this help his relationship with his children? Primarily, it releases him from his need to be defensive. He will be able to interact with his children from a confident position of open and outstretched arms instead of a defensive posture of clenched fists.

Will the annoying idiosyncrasies improve with time? Possibly. Possibly not. But which would you rather have: a husband who has finally stopped dropping his dirty clothes on the floor but who is distant, or a husband who feels accepted enough in his home that he can interact with you and the kids freely, without a need to be defensive? Accepting idiosyncrasies is a matter of choosing to focus on what is really important.

Accept His Family History

Depending on his age and the date of your marriage, I would venture to say that your husband has spent less than half of his life with you. For the majority of his life, he was part of another family, and he learned to do things the way they were done in that family. His table manners reflect his first family's table manners. He chooses vacation spots where they chose theirs. He plays out his "role" according to how his father played out his.

Of course there are exceptions, but you've probably found that the same is true of you. Your family history is different from his. And sometimes "different" may seem more like "wrong" to you. The differences he brings into your relationship will add new dimensions to your new family. This can be good. It's not right or wrong to open Christmas presents on Christmas Eve, as I discovered after Judd and I were married. It was simply different from what my family had done, and it took some getting used to. We learned to adapt to both traditions, having our "real Christmas service" after the presents. Adaptability brings creative possibilities into the relationship—and it can even be fun.

Beyond the simple "inherited" idiosyncrasies (like what I've been describing), your husband carries with him into his fathering the more serious history of a healthy family or a struggling family. Sadly enough, it is no longer the norm for a man to have a healthy family experience to look back on and learn from as he works out his own fathering style. He may have suffered through the breakdown of his parents' marriage. Maybe his own father neglected him, and he has never experienced the benefits of a healthy father-son relationship. He may have come from a family of con artists, welfare abusers, or drug addicts.

Whether your husband comes from a difficult background or simply seems to have brought with him too many of those "different" family traditions, it is extremely important that he feels accepted for who he is at the moment, with all of the potential given to him by a loving God. As he is able to break from his unhealthy past with God's help, and through your shelter of acceptance, love, and prayers, his interaction with his own children will blossom into a healthy relationship modeled upon God's Word.

What is it that your husband would ask of you if he were given the chance? What does he need in his home environment to encourage him to be a present, productive, and nurturing father? If his natural tendency is to be defensive, a sense of acceptance will encourage him to lay down his arms, put aside the masks that he often wears in the workplace and his social world, and be himself, accept himself, and in turn accept his children.

A Shelter of Comfort

One of the best ways to encourage your husband's fathering is to help him get out of his head, out of his habits, and into his heart. Recently, author Larry Crabb urged men to live by *courage* (from their hearts) instead of by *codes* (based on their habits).[1]

The comfort we offer can assist them in that. *Comfort* is the word I use to describe actively loving our husbands so that their hearts are opened. And if we are able to connect them with their emotional side, they will be much more inclined to turn their hearts toward their children.

What is it that makes your husband *feel* loved? It will differ for each man. In Judd's book *How Do You Say "I Love You"?* his premise is that everyone expresses and understands love in different "love languages." Maybe you express love verbally or through physical touch, but your husband doesn't feel loved unless he feels you are on his side when it comes to disciplining the kids. Maybe his way of saying "I love you" is to make sure you have a nice home and your material needs are met, but you aren't picking up his message, because if he really loved you he'd help more around the house. If you truly want to say "I love you" and have your husband understand your love for him, you have to learn his language. Judd writes about me:

> Nan is a mover of furniture. I never know from one month to the next where I will find my favorite chair. One week it will be in the dining room, the next in the living room and the following in our bedroom. When she begins the monthly migration, she is on cloud nine if I help her. She has a task she enjoys, and when I help with the heavy part, she feels like the most beloved lady in the land. Caring about what's important to Nan shows I care about Nan.[2]

Comfort is expressed in the little ways we show our love. I have learned in our household that in order for Judd to feel like his world is stable, in order for him to feel comfort, I need to perform a few simple tasks. I discovered his areas of comfort when I went back to school and then to work. Judd could put up with some cobwebs in the corners and an occasional unmade bed (issues that were anathema to my father, and so I had assumed to all men), but if his socks weren't matched, if he didn't have several clean shirts to wear, if he had to make his own lunch, or if dinner was a frozen pizza more than one night a week, Judd began to feel discomfort!

Once we realized what made each of us feel loved and cared for, we were able to make the necessary adjustments. On my part, if the dishes weren't done *and* the laundry needed to be folded, I made sure to do the laundry first. Judd has never seemed to mind dirty dishes in the sink, so I've learned to adjust to his priorities. Providing him with clean shirts, matched socks, frozen leftovers stuck away for a microwaved lunch, and some good home cooking spell comfort to Judd at this point in our lives, and performing these elementary tasks gives me a sense of being a loving servant to my husband.

Every man is different. For some men, comfort may mean a half hour of quiet to give Dad a chance to unwind after work, or an evening in front of the television. For some "chef" husbands, it may mean free rein in the kitchen cooking up a favorite recipe. For others it may mean a tidy, well-kept house. For most it means not inundating them with the day's problems the second they walk in the door. Discover what helps your husband feel a sense of comfort in his own home, and then do your best to help him achieve that comfort.

The Comfort of Sex

For all men there seems to be a comfort his wife gives that probably outshines all else. This is the comfort of sexual relations. For most of us wives, who are comforted by kind and compassionate words, cuddling, candles, and soft music, it may always remain a mystery why a man's needs cannot be the same. But the truth is, they are not.

I was struck by a recent Associated Press release from Tokyo. Apparently, after denying it for decades, the Japanese

government acknowledged that the army had recruited
Asian women to provide sex for the Japanese troops during
World War II. Ironically, these women were referred to as
"comfort women," which is an unfortunate twist to the
intended "comfort" that a wife can give to her beloved. But
some sort of statement was being made: In the rigors of the
"wars" men fight, sex is seen as comfort.

God's amazing plan for sexual intercourse provides the
opportunity for a connectedness that goes far beyond the
physical union of husband and wife. In this union, the two
"differents" become one. Perhaps because the wife is typically the emotional side of the team, it is through this union
that the husband is able to become more in touch with the
passionate and feeling side of his nature.

Solomon is frequently quoted by theologians when
describing the joy of a sexual relationship: "Drink from your
own well, my son—be faithful and true to your wife. . . .
Rejoice in the wife of your youth. Let her [charms] and tender embrace satisfy you. Let her love alone fill you with
delight" (Proverbs 5:15, 18-19, TLB).

Our charms and tender embrace will begin the comfort
process of a healthy sexual relationship. Do you think of
yourself as charming? Tender? After a tough day with tod-
dlers or running the rat race at work, "charming" may be
the last word we'd use to describe ourselves!

I don't think we have to put on an act for our husbands.
It's usually quite difficult to act what we don't feel, and we
don't have to pretend that we feel "charming" for our husbands. Charm, in a godly sense, goes much deeper. It is
rooted in the original commitment we made to our husbands
and to God, and goes beyond the day-to-day ups and downs
of our feelings. We *can* take him into our arms and "fill him
with delight" and the comfort of our sexuality because of the

long-lasting and far-reaching depth of our devotion to him
and to God.

I recently had coffee with Kathy, a wonderful, giving servant of God who has three very young children. On this particular morning she was deeply troubled. She had just
finished a demanding week of vacation Bible school, and her
husband, a usually tender and caring father, had become pre-
occupied with an emergency project on the house. Instead
of having a week of recuperation after Bible school, she was
faced with a torn-up house and three children to entertain
day and night by herself.

Kathy felt physical and emotional "burnout," while her
husband, who was energized by the creative challenge of his
remodeling efforts, could not understand why Kathy would
not respond to his sexual advances. "I can't give anymore,"
she responded tearfully, and they talked about her feelings.
Because she so desperately wanted to be a giving wife, she
felt devastated that she simply had no more to give.

As we talked, I could sense her fear that this might
become a pattern, and that she had failed her husband.
Sometimes, like Kathy, we tend to define ourselves by what
we feel at the moment: "I could not give to my husband
today. Therefore, I am a hard-hearted, non-giving person,
and that's the way I will probably be tomorrow and for the
rest of my life." I assured her that she was not the only one
who had gone through such an experience; her relationship
with her husband was not in jeopardy because of one
instance. She was right to confess her feelings to her husband in complete and total honesty, and there were no
unhealthy patterns developing in their marriage. It had simply been a very difficult week.

Kathy's "burnout" from giving to her family all day long is
not unusual among young mothers. When, however, we begin

to see a pattern emerging—many sudden "headaches,"
always too tired, or using "no" as a way of punishing our husbands—that is when we need to do some serious soul searching. That is the time to apply 1 Corinthians 13 to the sexual
relationship. It is God working within you who will help you
apply these attributes of love. You can become patient and
kind; never envious or jealous; not possessive; not conceited
or rude; never indiscreet; never insisting on your own way;
never hypersensitive or resentful; paying no attention to a suffered wrong; never counting up past wrongs; always believing
the best of your husband. You *can* be all of this because of
God's unfailing love working within you.

Room to Fail

Let's take a moment for a reality check, a reminder that we
will never furnish exactly the kind of environment our husbands need. But whether we're conscious of it or not, every
day we are creating an environment of some kind in our
homes.

Trying to create the perfect environment is an overwhelming task. None of us is perfect; you will fail at times,
just as your husband fails from time to time. That's okay. A
lifetime commitment is too long to go without being able to
make mistakes. Allow yourself to make mistakes, get up,
straighten yourself, dust yourself off, and start again.

It is important to see the little boy in your husband, not to
treat him like a child, but to recognize that it comforts him
when you meet his needs—and some of those needs will be
very close to the ones he had when he was little. As the
mother of grown sons, I pray that when they marry, their
wives will be able to see and love the little boy I knew and
loved through the years.

Providing a shelter for your husband does not belittle his

leadership, but actually affirms and equips him to be the best "healed" leader he can be. Your reward will be a husband who feels honored and respected, accepted and loved, and you will have laid the groundwork for his involvement in your home.

Questions for Personal Reflection

Think about these before discussion group.

1. Name one characteristic, mannerism, or trait that you have learned to accept in your husband. How has he been encouraged by this?

2. What are some issues that are difficult to confront your husband with?

Questions for Discussion

To discuss with a small group

1. How can you confront your husband and still let him know that you accept him?

2. How have you learned your husband's "love language"? In what ways do you provide comfort for him?

3. Do you feel overwhelmed by the task of being the caretaker of the emotional environment of the family? How do you think a good balance can be reached in this area?

13 Give Him Space

Most mothers love to hover. I suspect it's not that we love the worry and care hovering entails, but that we can barely help ourselves. It seems to be a component of our nature. At one time our children were a part of our bodies. In the womb they were safe; we took them everywhere we went; we were the ones to feed them, shelter them, and protect them. These babies were our full possession and responsibility.

Then came the traumatic separation of birth. That tiny being was no longer quite so totally ours. We loosened our grasp and shared with another adult the nurturing and care-taking of a separate person who was once part of ourselves. What a relief to share the responsibilities! And yet . . . it was also difficult to share in a way, because it meant letting go a little of the affirming sense that we know better than anyone else in the world what our babies, small or grown, need and deserve. And, were we to be totally honest, we *still* treasure that unique connection that we as mothers experience with each of our children.

So we hover. We try to be there to fix anything that goes wrong. We anticipate problems, and already have the solutions worked out so we can direct anyone else involved in how to solve the problem. We become supermoms. Occasionally we end up turning down the offered assistance of the well-meaning dad because, well, we've "got things covered."

Recently Judd and I were sitting on the porch of a cafe down near the bottom of the Grand Canyon. We had hiked into the Havasupai Indian reservation to spend a few days basking in the beauty of the untouched canyon, with its breathtaking waterfalls and clear rushing streams. One of the highlights of the trip was to witness the simple life-style of the Indians, and to observe their communal style of living that was so refreshing and inviting compared to our very individualistic and materialistic society.

We were intrigued by the scene played out before us as we sat on the porch of the cafe that morning. Two Havasu Indian mothers were sitting at separate tables. From the banana peels and empty water bottles on the table it was evident that they had eaten and were apparently now being entertained by the helicopter that flew in and out of the canyon with its monthly load of perishables. Four little children were playing with an empty box and another small object, which two children suddenly desired at the same time.

As we watched the drama unfold, we were shocked to see one of the sweet-faced little children give a vicious kick to the smaller one's abdomen. The little guy screamed in pain and rage. My motherly instincts sprang to life, but I restrained myself and waited to see how the mothers of these little warriors would respond.

The wounded, sobbing toddler hurried over and crawled up beside his mother, who continued to watch the heliport in sober contemplation. Apparently she had the view that children aren't as fragile as we think they are. Sure enough, the child comforted himself and stopped crying. Pretty soon he noticed us sitting there and began to entertain us by making noises and faces and then laughing contagiously. At the sound of his laughter, his mother turned to him and began to tussle his hair and poke at him affectionately.

I don't understand the philosophy behind child rearing in the Havasupai tribe, but from other incidents we observed while in the canyon, it was obvious that hovering was not a problem with these mothers. It was evident in the way the mothers trusted their children to solve some of their own problems, and it was evident in the way the mothers trusted the fathers.

Although these mothers were always present and available, I got a distinct sense that they were never overprotective or possessive with their children. On one walk up from the waterfalls, we passed a father sitting with his children as they played in the water and tumbled in the dirt. The children were a vital part of the community and were safe within the boundaries of the tribe. Because the mothers did not put a wall around their children, the children had the valuable involvement of many people in their lives. The African proverb "It takes a whole village to raise a child" appears to be true in the Havasupai nation as well.

"If you want something done right, you've got to do it yourself" may be a more accurate proverb for our American culture. In our individualistic society, we find it difficult to let go and trust that others can love our children and do what is best for them.

I believe God intends for the family to live in community, and the most intimate expression of that community is the father, mother, and children. We as mothers must stop hovering and allow our husbands to also instruct and nurture our children.

What does this look like in practical terms? It means giving him space—space to make mistakes, space to make decisions, space to develop his own unique relationship with his children.

Give Him Space to Make Mistakes

Janet, a young newlywed, had high expectations for her husband. When their first child was born, she taught the new father how to change diapers, how to hold him, how to feed little Stuart without getting any food on the floor, how to dress him, and how to talk to him. There was one right way—*her way.*

The poor young father, desperately wanting to be involved in the nurturing of his new son, tried in his bungling ways to relate to the baby under all the conditions set by his knowledgeable wife. When John held Stuart in his arms the new infant's head rolled and bobbed; mother would rescue the baby with alarm. When Dad changed Stuart's diapers, they bulged and gaped; mother complained and redid them. When Dad fed the baby, Mother hovered over the pair, making sure he held the bottle right and that he burped the baby at the right intervals.

Choosing outfits for Stuart to wear on Sunday morning was definitely not in Dad's area of expertise. His approach was, if it fit, it was fine. One sight of her baby's regalia and mother, quickly anticipating what others would think of her precious little one's appearance, grabbed the "right" outfit and slipped it on before leaving for church.

Ouch! We are all guilty of making some of the same mistakes this young mother made. *We* know how it should be done. *We* are the experts at child rearing. After all, who taught fathers how to parent? In most cases, we did. Some of us are with our children all day long, we know the proper way to handle them, and we're more observant when it comes to fashion. Why can't a father be more like a mother? We are perfectly willing to train them!

Through her actions, Janet communicated a number of

messages. She certainly communicated her great commitment to her child and her desire that Stuart receive the best parenting she and John could offer. But John also heard a less benevolent message: "John, I don't trust you with Stuart. Your intentions may be good, but I don't think you're equipped to handle this little person. I can show you how to do it right, but otherwise you'll just have to let me take care of him."

This was not what John wanted from his wife, and it's not what our husbands want from us. For all our good intentions, our hovering will only discourage them from being involved at all with their children. On a National Center for Fathering survey, one man wrote, "She wouldn't let me help with the kids in the earlier years, from birth to age three." It's easy for us to fall into this trap while the children are young. And it's easy for fathers to give up, to say to themselves, "Babies aren't my strong suit," and wait until they can teach their sons to play baseball or take their daughters to the movies. Before we know it, we're telling our husbands, "You need to spend more time with your son (or daughter)." The husbands feel like they've gotten mixed messages. And by the time the children do grow older, if fathers have had no history of intimate interaction, it's very difficult to start.

Your daughters particularly suffer if you do not step aside to encourage interaction with their dad. A father can usually catch up with his sons as they grow older, but how can he ever understand his daughters if he has little contact with them for the first few years of their lives? Many men feel very threatened when their daughters change from a girl into a woman, and if the window for your husband's involvement is not open from the time of your daughter's birth, it may stay forever shut. (See appendix A for more on fathers and daughters.)

Admittedly, our difficulty in letting go is largely due to our husbands' occasional mistakes. But we have to ask ourselves whether *our* way is necessarily the only right way—and answer *honestly.* Ken quoted pediatrician Mark Sands earlier: "Dads don't want to be told, 'I need help with this, but I want it done *this* way.' If a mother wants help in getting a child to sleep, it may not be best for her to instruct her husband to keep the child in the crib and pat him to sleep. The father may want to walk the baby. He wants to problem-solve too."

Dr. Sands further comments: "Fathers have to explain to their wives that they relate differently. They may diaper or feed differently, but as long as it's effective and gets the job done, does it really matter?"[1]

Does it really matter?

Sands' idea of "problem solving" is worth noting. Perhaps by not letting our husbands make mistakes, we cut them off from one of the joys they find in fathering: namely, acquiring the wisdom to do one of the most important jobs in the world, and do it well. Yet right on through all the stages of our children's development, we overprotect to try to shield them from the bumbling and seemingly unsophisticated attempts of inexperienced fathers. And our husbands continue to think of themselves as just that: bumbling, unsophisticated, and inexperienced.

Give Him Space to Make Decisions

Recently I had a conversation with Diane, a young mother who was deliberating over whether or not to home school her children. Her Christian friends were all home schooling, some because they had become disenchanted with the public school system, others because they felt that it was the parent's God-ordained directive, and still others because of fear of what might become of their children in a humanistic and sinful environment. Diane felt pressured to conform to their standards.

Fearful that her children were being irreversibly damaged by going to public school, Diane pleaded with her husband to allow her to home school. However, George, a devout Christian and loving father, would not agree to take the children out of their public schools. He believed that the children were safe and could grow and be lights in their non-Christian classrooms.

Diane faced a dilemma. Were her children's Christian values and futures at stake because of the stubbornness of her husband? Was she being faithful to her children? Did she know what was best—better than her husband?

There were two approaches she could take. One would be to insist on doing it her way. This would give her the power and the control in deciding what was best for her children. I'm afraid that very often this is the approach that we wives take. Since we are the primary caretakers of our children, we insist on doing it our way. Thus we drown out the unique wisdom our husbands have to offer and in effect block their involvement in our children's lives.

The second approach Diane could take would be to allow her husband to have the final word in the matter. They have already discussed the issue, he has heard her side, and still he believes his approach is right. Accepting a husband's decision in a case like this can be very frightening, especially when it comes to the precious lives of our children. How can we trust the wisdom of a father who is not around the children as much as we are, and who doesn't process information the same as we do?

It is exactly in this process of submission that I believe God's faithfulness is brought into the marriage relationship. We are asked to submit to our husbands (Ephesians 5:22) not because they possess superior wisdom, but for the sake of obedience to Christ. The matter becomes one of theology.

I have especially appreciated James Hurley's comments on this subject in his book *Man and Woman in Biblical Perspective*. When agreement cannot be reached in a particular situation even after discussion, prayer, and consultation with others, Hurley suggests a dialogue between husband and wife which goes something like this:

> Husband: Not because I am inherently wiser or more righteous, nor because I am right (although I do believe I am or I would not stand firm), but because it is finally my responsibility before God, we will take the course which I believe right. If I am being sinfully stubborn, may God forgive me and give me the grace to yield to you.
>
> Wife: Not because I believe you are wiser in this matter (I don't) or more righteous, nor because I accept that you are right (because I don't or I would not oppose you), but because I am a servant of God who has called me to honour your headship, I willingly yield to your decision. If I am wrong, may God show me. If you are wrong, may he give you grace to acknowledge it and to change.[2]

Something good happens in the relationship when we adopt a biblical perspective. First, we learn to trust God ultimately to honor his promise that "in all things God works for the good of those who love [and therefore obey] him, who have been called according to his purpose" (Romans 8:28, NIV). God has a purpose in setting up the system the way he did. By letting go of our own desires or ideas of what may be best, we learn to trust God as we expectantly wait to see what the outcome will be. In other words, by giving our husbands space to make decisions, we also give God space to show his protection and goodness.

The biggest disagreement that Judd and I ever had was over my going back to work. Because I wanted to right every wrong I felt I had experienced as a child, I felt very, very strongly that I should be available to my children and concentrate my energies on our family and its functions. As a family we had decided to use our farm as an outreach and ministry, and were constantly involved in activities taking place in our home. I was content with my life and felt it was already filled to the brim. Judd listened to me, understood my feelings—but still he wanted me to go to work.

The thought of getting an outside job struck more than fear in me. Even though our children were all in school, in my mind it meant that our family was going to disintegrate. I would not be there when they needed me. How could I possibly add a job to all the things I was now doing?

I thought God would bail me out. Judd felt we needed more money, so I prayed for more money. I went to the mailbox every day, honestly expecting to find some donor check or a sweepstakes prize or an inheritance . . . something from God. My next strategy was to pray that God would change Judd's mind, and if you knew my husband, you'd realize that I was praying for a miracle! Judd is a German who knows what he wants and goes for it. Actually that is one thing I have always loved about him, but now this trait of his rubbed the wrong way! I knew that God could work miracles—but he didn't. Judd still wanted me to go to work.

I was in a quandary. I knew that God would have me submit to my husband. I knew that a loving God could have res-
cued me. But he hadn't. So I began the process of going
back to work.

And I watched God's miracles. I enjoyed working. I found
jobs that gave me flexible hours so I could be home with the
children. The housework still got done, and my family did
not fall apart. When the boys graduated from high school,
they each stood before our church at the baccalaureate service and thanked me for "always being there when they
needed me." And I thanked God that he had been faithful
when I needed him, when I was frightened of my role of submission and honor.

Along with honoring God, submitting to the desires or the
decisions of your husband sends him several messages. You
are telling him first of all that you desire to serve God, and
second, that his leadership is intact. This will help him recognize how vital his involvement is in your family. It will also
challenge him to maintain a close relationship with God as
he makes important family decisions, and give him space to
carry out the heavy mandate of headship of the family.

Give Your Family Space to Grow Together

When our boys were small, Judd loved to take them out on
"manly" adventures such as climbing and hiking. We lived in
southern California at the time, and there were wonderful
climbing areas where the guys loved to go for challenging
hikes. Some of my greatest intercessory prayers were
offered after packing a lunch for my mighty warriors and
watching them swagger out to the car, full of three- and four-
year-old confidence in this idol who would lead them out to
conquer whatever challenges lay before them. Several hours
later they would return, dirty, sweaty, and tired, but with

wonderful adventure tales to tell (horrific tales to a mother's
ears) of falling, almost drowning, or of coming "close to the
edge of certain death." From their jubilance I could tell that
they had taken one more step closer to manhood, closer to
becoming like the Hero-Dad, and the father-son bond was
drawn a little tighter.

My struggle and my responsibility were to stand aside,
trusting God's care of my "babies" as they spent time in
their own special adventures with their dad. *Judd is the man
God has chosen to be the father of my children.* His qualities
need to rub off on his children, and this happens only when
they share the great and the not-so-great times. In order for
God's purposes to be fulfilled in these father and son relationships, I needed to allow time and room for them to build
their unique relationships.

Our boys are in their early twenties now, and we are reap-
ing the rewards of our dual parenting. Recently, a friend who
had invited Dan and his fiancée over for dinner remarked to
me, "I got such enjoyment out of visiting with Dan. First I
would see something that he did or said, and I would say to
myself, *That's Judd.* Then he would do something else and
I'd think, *That's Nancy.* It was fun to sit back and see how
your two personalities and characters merge in your son."
Our boys are very much their own persons, with their own
desires to serve God, and it has been rewarding to watch
how they've benefited from (and been challenged by) the
influences of both Judd and me.

Judd has had to adapt to our daughter, Sara, who is quite
nonaggressive and likes reading, walking, and quiet activities. I have enjoyed watching them develop their own way of
relating. Sara giggles at her dad when he gets a little loud
and dogmatic, and she can usually help him see her point of
view in a sweet and nonthreatening way. This summer the

two of them took an Amtrak trip from Kansas City to St.
Louis since Sara had never ridden a train. I got left at home,
but knowing that these two people I love found pleasure in
being together and were building special memories compen-
sated for any feeling of being left out.

We mothers can encourage fathers by standing aside and
allowing just Dad and the children to enjoy these special
times together. It gives our children the time to bond, to
learn to emulate characteristics they see in their dad, and to
discover who they are in relationship to him.

If our purpose is to share the parenting role as a total and
complete team, a team that is made up of complements, not
antagonists, then we must accept the talents and viewpoints,
the weaknesses and vulnerabilities of our companion. We
need to see that there are different ways of achieving the
same purposes, and learn to step aside to give him space so
he can relate to his children with his own personality and in
his own way.

Questions for Personal Reflection

Think about these before discussion group.

1. In what ways do you tend to hover over your children? Can you
identify the feelings that prompt this hovering? How does hovering
hinder your husband from being the father he can be?

2. How can you help well-meaning mothers learn their boundaries so
they don't overwhelm the father and take away some of his
God-given contributions to his children?

3. What has your husband done with or for his children that has embarrassed you or frustrated you? How did you react? What did you learn?

Questions for Discussion

To discuss with your husband and/or a small group

1. Which characteristics of your husband would you like to see in your children? How can you encourage this type of modeling?

2. What is one of the tough decisions that you have had to yield to your husband as it relates to your children? What was the outcome?

3. What particular activities do your children enjoy doing with their father?

4. What can you do to encourage your husband to spend time doing things with his children? Do these activities necessarily have to be outings, or can they be chores, reading stories, etc.?

14 Give Him Feedback

Judd and I were sitting in the audience waiting for the concert to begin. It was a bluegrass band: guitar, banjo, mandolin, and fiddle. The guitarist adjusted his microphone while the others tuned their instruments.

The guitarist leaned into the mike: "Test, one, two, three . . . test." And then suddenly—ouch! That sound!

You've heard it before. The huge speakers screeched and a high, piercing wail assaulted our eardrums. The guitarist jumped back from the mike. Throughout the audience people clapped their hands over their ears. The sound technician flew into action.

We call it feedback, and it is not a pleasant experience.

Before long the concert began. "A-one, two, three, four," the guitarist said, and the band kicked into a high-powered bluegrass tune that seemed to be written entirely in sixteenth notes. I was amazed that the band members could keep up with each other. But they blended their talents beautifully. Hands that a few minutes ago were clapped over ears now clapped in time to the music.

We were witnessing a different kind of feedback. Through monitors facing toward them, the band received feedback on how they sounded to the audience. Because of those monitors, we were listening to beautifully synchronized music.

Two kinds of feedback: one type that was harsh and deafening, the other that created music pleasant to the ears.

This experience captures the two ways we wives can give feedback to our husbands. We can catch our husbands doing something wrong and beat them over the head with it—giving feedback that is harsh and critical. "Can't you do anything right?" we screech. Our criticism assaults their senses, and they cover their ears to block out our words. They jump back from us and from their children, and do not perform.

Has the word *feedback* taken on purely negative connotations? I hope not. There is a positive type of feedback which is like the music streaming through a monitor. Instead of harsh criticism, we can simply "reflect back" to our husbands what they need to know about their fathering. When your husband is playing beautiful music as a father, you reflect that beautiful music back to him through praise and positive feedback. "You know," you tell him, "I think you handled that situation really well with Brian. I think he learned his lesson and felt loved at the same time. Good job." Sometimes we forget that a monitor lets the musician enjoy the concert, too.

A monitor also informs a musician about what the audience is experiencing. In the same way, we wives can give our husbands feedback by letting them know what's going on in their children's lives and minds. Perhaps there is news your husband hasn't heard yet: "Jackie's going to try out for a part in the drama department play. I think she's nervous." Other times, there are perceptions your husband didn't pick up: "I think Samuel was hurt by what you said at dinner. He didn't finish his meal."

Related to this is the way a monitor confronts the perceptive musician with his mistakes. If the sound was never reflected back to him, he might continue to play on, off beat or out of tune. But when the sound is repeated back to him so he can hear what he's been playing, he can make the necessary adjustments. There will be times when your husband's behavior is foolish or sinful, and thus destructive. For his own good, and the good of your family, he needs to be confronted about that behavior. Again, we can confront him in a way that encourages a man to stop, retune, and try again. We can also confront in ways that force him to jump back and plug his ears.

We wives can encourage our husbands to play beautiful music with their children when we act as monitors and give them good feedback. We can give monitor-like feedback in the three ways described above: by praising them for what they do right, by providing them information about their children, and by confronting them when necessary. Let's look at each in more detail.

Feedback through Praise and Encouragement

Fathers need to hear when they are doing things right.

The primary reason to praise our husbands when they do something right is that it conveys the honor which I described in an earlier chapter. Give honor when honor is due. Your husband's confidence will flourish; your love will be heard.

But again we confront the problem of those husbands who *seem* downright dishonorable. The times when we do catch them doing something right seem few and far between. And the praiseworthy things they do seem so minuscule in comparison to the other things they do that we wonder, "Why bother to praise it?" If a father has abandoned his children, should we nonetheless praise him for being faithful with his child support payments? Should we praise a father who works too much overtime because, on one occasion, he took thirty seconds to tie his daughter's shoe?

I teach freshman composition at a small college. Sometimes when I'm up late at night grading papers, I'll be reading through a student's essay, and a thought will run through my head: *Boy, this is really a bad piece of writing.* I'll reach for my red pen, ready to "whip this paper into shape," and then I'll remember what a writing professor told me back in grad school.

A study was done of students who received their papers back from their instructor. Researchers were interested in how students responded to comments on the page, and they found that for the most part, the students simply scanned the pages for the positive comments. They ignored the negative comments altogether, or came back to them later. The study advised instructors to employ only two types of critique: positive feedback and very specific instructions on how to correct particular problems in the paper. The students used such comments to improve their papers the second time around.

Regardless of whether you think positive feedback lets someone off the hook, the fact of the matter is that *praise works.* When your husband hears that he is doing something right, it makes him more likely to continue that behavior and to feel positive enough about his fathering that he will be freed to respond to his children more naturally and constructively.

Saturday was a day Jim always set aside to do yard work that he couldn't get to during the week. As he started up the lawn mower early Saturday morning, Brian, his three-year-old, came running out of the house with his little plastic lawn mower, anxious to tackle the tall grass just like Daddy. Linda, sipping her morning coffee, watched from the sliding glass doors as Jim hesitated and then patiently walked over to Brian, showing him his special place to mow right behind

Daddy. As Linda checked on them throughout the morning she was pleased to see that father and son were enjoying each other despite the many interruptions and slow progress of the lawn care.

By lunchtime, Jim was getting discouraged. He lingered over his sandwich, bemoaning all the work still to be done. But Linda gently reminded him of all he had accomplished that morning; investing time in his son was much more important than cutting grass that would only grow back again next week. She praised him for his choice to spend patient and loving time with his son, and for being a role model to a future father.

Through Linda's insight, Jim was encouraged, and his behavior reinforced. The next time a similar incident arises, Jim will have the benefit of Linda's perspective and will feel affirmed in his choice to place a relationship with his son above his work goals. We wives can encourage our husbands in their fathering practices as we recognize their strengths and express appreciation.

Your encouragement might seem small. Sharon's father never bought candy for his children or took them out for hamburgers, so whenever her husband Bill does these things for their kids, Sharon has always reminded them to say "thank you" for the treat. Bill has commented to me, "You know, their gratitude really is important to me, and it makes me want to do all the more for them."

As wives, we occupy the best seats to observe the interaction between our children and their father. We see the good things that happen, but for some reason—maybe because they are what we expected, or because we would like to see the good relationship as a natural, everyday occurrence—we don't say anything. Afraid that we'll somehow break the magic spell if we mention it, we keep our praise to ourselves.

A Wife's Encouragement Affects
Her Husband's Spiritual Leadership

Over 1,500 fathers were asked to rate their satisfaction level with their wives' support of their fathering. Fathers were asked to describe themselves as being dissatisfied (LOW), having mixed feelings (MED) or being satisfied (HIGH) with the support given to them by their wives. These three groups of fathers were then compared in their **Spiritual Leadership,** *as measured by the Personal Fathering Profile. The differences in the scores from each group are as follows:*

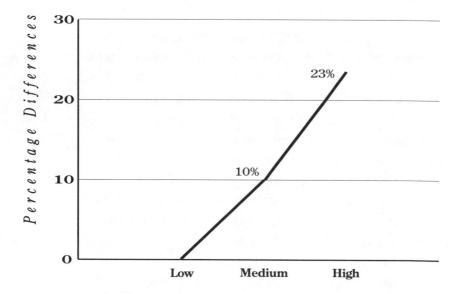

The more a husband senses your support of him as a father, the more likely it is that he will be a spiritual leader for his children.

A committed father encourages his children to grow spiritually by praying with them, reading the Bible with them, and actively leading their participation in a local church or parish. He discusses spiritual concepts with his children and leads them in applying these concepts daily.

He took time to read to Sam before bed last night; he came home early and played whiffle ball with the children in the backyard; at the dinner table he praised thirteen-year-old Lori for her first attempt at baking lasagna. His humor is something the children always enjoy, and he entertains them on the way to church. He quietly gets out his checkbook and writes out a check to cover the cost of a junior-high camping trip for Matt when you know he is wondering if he can pay all this month's bills. He awkwardly attempts to initiate a family prayer time in the evenings.

It is important that he feels recognized for the little things he does, and your praise will encourage him to continue.

Ken has expressed his concern for men in one of their biggest struggles: anything that has to do with spirituality. Perhaps it is difficult for men to express spirituality because it is so personal, and they are accustomed to relating objectively and intellectually. For whatever reason, our husbands need to be praised and encouraged in their spiritual headship. Encourage your husband to do the praying at mealtimes. Even if he doesn't have the flowery words of a seasoned pastor, join in with your heart. Thank him when he initiates a family devotional time; be there with conviction and support. Although he may not voice it, he may wonder, *Did I do it right?* Any attempt he makes in establishing spiritual leadership is honorable, and deserves to be encouraged by your words and your attitude. Encourage him, pray for him, and allow God to enrich his spiritual leadership.

Praise fires a powerful and direct attack on the five fathering fears. Praise attacks a sense of inadequacy by saying, "You are good at what you do." Praise attacks a sense of being left out by saying, "Look, you *are* fathering your child." For anger, praise says, "You are breaking the destructive patterns you inherited." For a sense of embarrassment, praise says, "Be proud of what you've done." For a sense of being all alone, praise says, "I'm with you and I'm your biggest fan."

Feedback through Information

The Puritans had a saying that in parenting "two eyes see more than one."[1] Another common epigram told fathers that "your wife is your eye to see when you are not there, she is your hand to touch, she is your ear to hear."

One of the four fathering tasks is awareness. You can help your husband be a more aware father by supplying him with information. What have you observed in the kids? What did you notice this morning at breakfast? What insight did you gain on the way home from school? Tell your husband.

The fact that you're with your children more hours than he is means that you possess certain information he has no other access to. If you work in the home, then you're around the kids for eight or nine hours during the day while your husband is at work. When he comes home from work, you can fill him in on the many things that have happened between breakfast and naptime. If you work outside the home, there are still times when you shuttle the kids to gymnastics and he picks them up from youth group. When you both arrive home, it's important to compare notes, like any good team.

There's another type of information you possess but your husband does not: your own unique perspective. He needs more than news; he needs your interpretation of what is going on under the surfaces of your children's lives. What are your daughter's gifts? What are your son's strengths and weaknesses? What especially encourages your child? What leaves him or her deflated?

I believe sensitivity to these kinds of things is part of a

mother's special gift. The mother is usually the one who has a finger on the pulse of the children's lives. She sees with her heart the little indications of self-doubt, the manifestations of a wounded spirit, the hint of depression. She feels with the children when their hearts are flying high or sinking into despair. Perhaps it is what Edith Stein describes as a woman's strength: ". . . the intuitive grasp of the living concrete; especially of the personal element. She has the special gift of making herself at home in the inner world of others."[2]

A man recognizes this ability women have to be intuitively connected to their children, and this intuition can be a threat to him—if his wife allows it to be. She can use this special gift as a weapon to exclude her husband from the "inner circle." If the wife uses her knowledge to exclude her husband, or if she condemns him for not "seeing" what she sees, a division will grow not only in the marriage but also in the relationship between father and children. If he feels inferior, like an outsider or a bumbling idiot, he won't want to "play the game" anymore, and he'll withdraw from the relationship and let the one "in the know" relate to the children.

On the other hand, as you share your insights with your husband, you give him needed knowledge that will allow him to more accurately adapt his fathering to his children's needs. Some of the best times for Judd and me to talk about the children came at night, after they had gone to sleep, and usually when we were resting quietly in bed. Those were the private times when I could relate to Judd some of my observations from the day, concerns that I had for one of the children, or a special breakthrough I had witnessed.

When one of the boys shared a particularly hurtful comment someone had made at school, when I observed Sara quietly growing in her faith, when Dan showed signs of his gift for working with children, when Derrick's defense of a

classmate showed compassion and empathy, I brought up all
of these events in our discussions. Once Judd heard my
observations concerning the day, we could discuss the impli-
cations and he could then interact with the children from a
standpoint of awareness. I also found that his reactions gave
me a new perspective on the issues.

As is true with most effective communication, timing is
key. If your husband is not a night owl, you may want to
avoid approaching him as he's getting ready for bed. Judd
does much of his thinking and processing of information as
he showers in the morning. We were a little slow to recognize that this was not a good time for me. Judd would come
out of the bathroom excitedly, dripping all over the bedroom
carpet. "Nancy, I think I've got it!" he would say, and then
he'd go on with his ideas. By ten o'clock in the morning,
when I was fully awake, I would have forgotten that we had
even talked, let alone what was said.

Some couples, especially those with little children, schedule dates with each other to go over what has happened in
the past week and make plans for the next. Others find that
after mealtime, when the children are playing, is the best
time to talk. Some couples take an entire weekend alone
together. They pack the kids off to Grandma's and take a
mini-vacation somewhere—not only to relax, but also to
review. "Okay, how do you think Johnny's doing?" they start
out.

However you do it, it's vital that each of you share your
perspectives about your children if you're to be a team that
nurtures and trains your kids.

Feedback through Confrontation

Confrontation is the third means of providing your husband
beneficial feedback.

David Augsburger wrote a book entitled *Care Enough to Confront*. Ken Canfield calls a wife's confrontation *"care-frontation."* The connection these two make between caring for our husbands and confronting our husbands is built on a number of ideas:

- It is natural for all of us to lapse into foolishly and sinfully destructive behavior.
- It is natural for us to be blind to such destructive behavior.
- Refraining from destructive behavior is good for the sinner as well as the sinned-against.

These statements lead us to a couple of conclusions:

- Confrontation is occasionally necessary, because we can be blind to our own actions.
- Appropriate confrontation is good, because it can free us to pursue the best course of action—God's commands.

Occasionally we all need to be confronted about something we have done or said. The confrontation is useful; otherwise, we might be like a blind person stumbling obliviously toward the edge of a cliff. We need someone to shout, "Wait! Stop! You're in great danger!" At such times, confrontation is an act of love and concern. Sometimes the best thing you can do for your husband is to tell him where he has gone wrong.

Does that contradict what I said earlier about giving him honor and praise? No. Remember, you give honor where honor is due. Here, you give censure where censure is due. But still, there are encouraging and effective ways to confront.

With the issue of confrontation, we have perhaps the biggest contrast in our analogy of feedback and monitors. There is a way to confront that is as harsh as the screech of a bad loudspeaker:

"If you had just paid attention, you would have known how overwhelmed she felt when you pushed her so hard to get on the volleyball team."

"How can you be so insensitive? He's already embarrassed about his blemishes, and now you have to scold him for not washing his face enough. He's been scrubbing morning, noon, and night."

"Why do you continually ignore the baby? He has been trying to get your attention and all you do is read the paper."

Are these wives speaking the truth? Are they accurately identifying destructive behavior? We can imagine situations where they are. Sometimes our husbands *are* inattentive. Sometimes they *are* insensitive. But regardless of how true these statements are, we can still smell the scent of "attack" in the way they have approached the confrontation.

When we attack fathers for their failures, they will feel inadequate and become unapproachable, or they will feel inferior and become the silent, insecure "almighty patriarch." At any rate, their defenses will prevent them from responding positively.

We wives get a lot of bad, stereotypical press for being nags. Have you ever had Proverbs 21:19 quoted to you? "It is better to live in a desert land, than with a contentious [nagging] and vexing woman." When we nag and vex, our husbands flee to safer territory. And when they clam up or run away, the cycle escalates because we sometimes think we have to be even more contentious to get through to them. Before long, our husbands have fled to a desert land. Their "desert" may be the newspaper or television, or late work hours, or a friend's house. But to them, it's preferable to home.

Scripture says that it is not enough simply to speak the truth; we must speak "the truth in love" (Ephesians 4:15). We must do what monitors do.

Monitors reflect the sound back to the musician, without attacking him or trying to show him what a lousy guitar player he is. They give him an accurate sense of what he is doing, so he can hear for himself the mistakes he is making and then, as he sees fit, change. We also need to lovingly reflect back to our husbands their destructive behavior.

Do you remember the story Ken told earlier about Stephen and Bethany? Bethany was the three-year-old daughter whom Sue (her mother) had encouraged to greet her dad at the door. Bethany would wait anxiously for Stephen to come home, and as his car pulled into the drive, she'd jump up and down and shout, "Daddy's home!" But Daddy would come in through the door and walk right past her, leaving Bethany trailing behind him. For the first few days, she was puzzled, but it wasn't long before she was dejected. Stephen's daughter felt crushed.

Because Sue cared about the relationship between her husband and daughter, she decided to confront Stephen about his insensitivity. But how she went about it reveals her wisdom. She "reflected back" to Stephen an accurate picture of what his actions were doing to Bethany.

"Steve, you ought to have seen Bethany's face when you walked on by. She thinks you're the most important man in the world, and I can tell she really has a hunger for your love. It hurts her when you walk by without paying any attention. I'm afraid there may come a time when she doesn't wait so anxiously for you to come home."

Stephen sat there and listened, appraising the situation.

He began to nod his head and make little "hmm" noises. "You're right," he said. The next day, when he came home from work, he caught little Bethany in his hands and swung her up toward the ceiling. She shrieked in delight.

Stephen listened to Sue's confrontation because she did it without attacking him. In fact, in some ways, she didn't focus on him at all. She focused on his behavior and on his daughter (whom he loves), and on the effects of his behavior. Stephen could analyze the situation with the new evidence he'd received, and then make his choice to change.

I'm also going to presume to comment on Ken's story from the first chapter: Remember the episode where he took his daughters on a dangerous wagon ride down a steep hill? When his wife, Dee, joined him, Ken said she "reflected back" to him the dangers of the ride. From her perspective up on the hill, she could see the small wagon careening along the concrete, with her daughters' little heads bouncing back and forth. Ken was blinded by the exhilaration of the moment, but Dee was more objective, and could share with him the information she possessed. She confronted him.

When you confront your husband, you are sharing your wider perspective with him, letting him see what he is doing. Usually it will be obvious why such behavior is wrong or harmful. You won't even have to tell him how careless or insensitive he has been, which is often the part that makes him defensive or pushes him away.

A monitor reflects sound back to the musician. Consequently, it is only as useful as it is accurate. In light of that fact, let me make three suggestions about giving accurate feedback to your husband.

1. Don't Confront If You Aren't Also Praising

In fact, your interaction with your husband should be characterized more by times of praise than by times of confrontation. "Has your wife ever discouraged you as a father?" the National Center for Fathering asked. "Yes," one man wrote, "she always points out what I didn't do." *Always?* Probably not, but it sure seems that way to this man.

Criticism without adequate and appropriate praise is hard to swallow. Part of the usefulness of a monitor is to let a musician hear what he *is* doing right, to let him enjoy the music that the audience is enjoying.

2. Give Specific Examples of Destructive Behavior

To reflect back destructive behavior is to let your husband *see* his destructive behavior. Maybe you are like me; I respond to feelings. If Judd told me, "I feel that you're hurting Sara in some of the things you say," I'd want to change, quick. But Judd (and I believe this is true of most men) wouldn't be so influenced if I said the same thing to him. Typically, men are inclined to operate on a more cognitive level; they are more comfortable dealing with the *facts*. We need to learn their language: "When you told Joey, 'You never do anything right,' I saw the color leave his face. Later I heard him repeat the same thing to himself when he dropped his knife at the dinner table. I know you didn't really mean it that way, but that's how it came across to him." Evidence through details and specific incidents is much better received than vague or emotional accusations.

It is not accurate to say, "You *always* neglect the kids." It is accurate to say, "I think David felt neglected when you didn't show up at his practice like you said."

3. Confrontation Should Be Appropriate to the Incident

We used to joke about those people who seemed to have read *Caring Enough to Confront* one too many times. We said, "They cared *too much.*" Some of the things our husbands do are not worth confronting him about, at least not at the moment. Some things require us to practice the other disciplines of an encouraging wife, namely, providing a shelter of acceptance or giving him space. We need to be wise about when and if to confront. It is possible to be too sensitive and carry confrontation too far.

But "appropriate" confrontations also work in the other direction. If your husband's destructive behavior is extreme, then so must be the confrontation. If your husband is abusive or otherwise puts your children in some serious danger, he needs to be confronted in a very strong manner. If he has beaten or physically harmed you in any way, he needs to be confronted by other people besides you. He may very well need to be confronted by the elders in your church or the law of the land.

Before this type of confrontation, you need to be convinced that it is the *very best* thing you can do for him. Unless he is confronted by the consequences of his behavior, he will end up destroying himself and all that he (deep down inside) considers important. The severity of his abuse is probably matched only by the depth of his blindness or lack of control. You can do for him what he cannot do for himself: confront his behavior as the first step in putting a stop to it.

Positive feedback can enhance a father's relationship with his children and his walk with his own Father, and it's both our duty and privilege as yokemates to offer it. We should not remain silent when we have the power and the insight to shed light on what is happening in relationships. Yet when we do speak, we must speak with love and a desire to see our husbands grow. We are not to use our knowledge as a means of bondage or as a weapon.

But what happens when our confrontations fail? Well, there may be other actions to take (especially in the case of abuse), but in all cases, we are called to forgive. That is the topic of my final chapter.

Questions for Personal Reflection

Think about these before discussion group.

1. What type of information do you feel is important to share with your husband?

2. What is one thing you have brought to your husband's attention about the children that has benefited them?

3. What area of your husband's fathering do you think is the most discouraging to him? How can you encourage him? A hug? Words? Prayer?

Questions for Discussion

To discuss with a small group

1. When is the best time for you and your husband to share observations and information about your children? Discuss with the group what you have found to be your best times for sharing.

2. How does your husband respond when he thinks you are nagging? What message does nagging give to the receiver?

3. With what area of confrontation do you find it hardest to take a positive approach? How can you confront in a successful way?

15 Forgive Him When Necessary

When I think of forgiveness, I am reminded of the time I almost killed my beloved yellow tabby.

Thomas has entertained us from his bottle-feeding days, when he fit into the palm of our hands, through six years of semimaturity. To save money, I had bought worm medicine from the local co-op and had successfully dewormed most of the domestic animals on the farm . . . except for Tom. The capsule broke in the cat's mouth, and he inhaled the near-lethal liquid into his lungs. Today Thomas gasps instead of breathes. He can no longer follow me around the farm while I do my chores. Yet, as he looks into my eyes, as he follows me around the house, as he welcomes me in the morning, I can see no trace of bitterness. He is still my faithful friend.

God's animal kingdom may give us object lessons on a very simplistic level, but when we translate them into our daily lives they can become powerful. Though the results of my mistake with Thomas cannot be erased, the relationship has been restored. I feel forgiven.

Freedom from grudges. Openness. Trust. Healing. Restoration. Unconditional love. Forgotten wrongs. All flow from forgiveness. A family that practices forgiveness is a family that will spread God's healing forgiveness beyond its boundaries into a world overcome by sin and guilt.

The Need for Forgiveness

Even within a small family unit, there is usually much to forgive. Inadequacies, mistakes, intentional offenses, and our
awareness of sins cause all of us to want to pull back from
each other, to erect walls of defense, to fight back. We inevitably experience these things in marriage, so God calls us to
practice forgiveness even when our best efforts at encouragement have gone unheeded. When we forgive our husbands we give them over to God, to whom they are
ultimately responsible, and we allow them space to make
mistakes, as I described earlier.

I remember one time when I had left nine-month-old Sara
with Judd for a few hours while I went to some early-morn-
ing garage sales with my sister. When we returned several
hours later, a careful search for father and daughter found
them on the back patio, Judd sound asleep on a lounge chair,
and little Sara sitting by a large flowerpot gingerly stuffing
potting soil into her mouth.

After waking Judd and cleaning our mud-faced baby, I was
reassured that she was none the worse for her interesting
diet. Seeing Judd's concern, I was convinced that he would
be more alert on his next tour of duty, and I forgave him his
negligence. We even had a few chuckles before we moved
on to other issues of the day. Because I forgave him, the
next time I chose to put all doubts behind me and once
again entrust my little girl to her father. Had I not been able
to forgive Judd, I think he would have backed off from his
attempts to be involved with his daughter.

Forgiving mistakes can be relatively easy. When a person
makes a mistake there is usually no forethought of malice or
intended harm. Everyone makes mistakes, and we need to
give our husbands space to make (and learn from) their

share. But if the only anecdotes that come to mind are of cleaning potting soil out of a baby's mouth, then I would be trivializing potentially dangerous patterns.

There are times when forgiveness is difficult. Maybe the offense was no mere mistake, but a calculated cruelty, and the result may not simply be an inconvenience, but a disruption of your lives. What were once isolated incidents may have become commonplace; your husband may not be repentant about what happened—in fact, he may even revel in it.

Very recently, Ken Canfield received a call at the National Center from a woman who now, after fourteen years of marriage, has become a single mother. "Oh grow up, Shari," her husband told her one day. "I don't love you anymore; I love Lisa. You're so immature." And with that he left her to marry his mistress.

Some of us hurt deeply. What about the father who has put work ahead of his kids? "Listen, don't bug me about the ball game tonight. I've got work to do. He'll do fine without me." What about the father who is abusive, or the husband who's unfaithful? Indeed, forgiveness can be very difficult.

There are situations in which it would be wise and righteous for you to take decisive action. For example, in an abusive situation it would be best to confront your husband, seek outside support, and find a safer environment for your children. (See appendix E for more specific help on abusive fathers.) But whatever other actions God would have us take, *he would also have us obey his command to forgive.*

Even when we're not in such difficult situations, it can be easy to make never-ending lists of all there is to forgive in our husbands. He's gone too much, and leaves you with all the parenting responsibility. He never wants to talk when you need to. He is always pushing you and the kids to perform rather than letting things be. He doesn't try to understand you. He avoids the list you made of things that need to be fixed around the house. When you tell him something is wrong, he withdraws, gets defensive, or counterattacks.

When there's no healthy pattern of forgiveness, this list can build up until no room is left for love, only grudges and harsh feelings. I've seen women become bitter and blame their husbands for anything that goes wrong in the family. We forget that this bitterness flows over into the lives of the children and colors their picture of their father. The "comical" nagging wife is a caricature of the woman who concentrates on the faults and never sees hope.

I have also seen wives give up, and settle into a relationship where they have simply chosen to ignore the anger and disappointment. They no longer expect anything, hope for anything; they merely withdraw into an uncomfortable silence.

Yet despite all the pain many of us feel, we are commanded to forgive others as God has forgiven us. Sometimes forgiveness seems impossible because we carry a misconception of what forgiveness is. Forgiveness is *not* permission to hide our heads in the sand and ignore the problem. The deed has happened; hiding our eyes will not make it go away. Forgiveness does not make the matter any less important. You were hurt, your children were hurt, trust was broken. The course of your lives has been altered to some slight or great degree, and that is very significant.

Forgiveness is a conscious act that takes into consideration the "humanness" of the other person. It is unconditional; without dwelling on the offense or dredging up past wrongs, it seeks to understand.

Recently I was reminded of my own weakness when it comes to forgiving. I felt that a great wrong had been done, and I was so angry I could not settle the problem in a Christlike manner. As I backed away to reexamine my own heart, I saw the wall between myself and the other person, and I cried out to God to help me tear it down. During my time of waiting upon the Lord, I remembered a line in a song that I had sung years before: "He looked beyond my guilt and saw my need."

I needed to look on the situation with *his* eyes, to see beyond my anger at the deed and understand the need that was being expressed through it. God's grace opened my eyes finally to see the need, and then respond with compassion.

Once we forgive, the walls are torn down and a bridge to healing is built.

The Power of Forgiveness

Judd and I enjoy reunions with our extended families. Through the years, we have witnessed many various offenses, young ones who have stepped outside of the Christian standards set by their parents, and disagreements about how things should be done. Yet, when we all come together to celebrate our common roots, there is an overwhelming sense of love and acceptance for all. And we have seen the healing that this atmosphere of forgiveness has brought to those "offenders," for many of them have come back into the circle of love provided by the family.

Why did God place such a high priority on forgiveness? How can it help our husbands become more effective fathers?

When we walk in a spirit of forgiveness, we take a giant leap toward breaking the barriers that can form around relationships. Forgiven fathers will enter into the community of the family as humble men who are able to acknowledge their own vulnerability and weakness, overcome their feelings of guilt and inadequacy, and open their lives to their kids. Forgiven fathers will be able to forgive their children, and not force them to live under unrealistic expectations.

When you forgive your husband, you convey to your children, "I love your father," and they draw strength from the security of that commitment. You create an atmosphere in which the children know they will also be extended forgiveness when they do wrong. You accept your husband, and your children understand that they will be accepted, too. And of course, your attitude of forgiveness provides a positive model for your children. Despite what may have happened to you, wouldn't it be much better to demonstrate to your children a quick tendency to forgive rather than to keep holding on to your bitter grudges?

Scripture addresses many promises that come with a forgiving heart. Forgiveness brings a natural response of love (Luke 7:42-43); it releases our prayers and keeps them from being hindered (1 Peter 3:7); it is a shield that keeps Satan from outwitting us (2 Corinthians 2:7-11).

The apostle Paul links forgiveness and encouragement together in Ephesians 4:29-32 (NIV):

> Do not let any unwholesome talk come out of your mouths, but only what is helpful for building others up according to their needs, that it may benefit those who listen. . . . Get rid of all bitterness, rage and anger, brawling and slander, along with every form of malice. Be kind and compassionate to one another, forgiving each other, just as in Christ God forgave you.

Forgiveness is a healing force that fosters encouragement and resolves conflicts. When we truly forgive our husbands, we restore their sense of wholeness, and their confidence will be reflected in their interaction with our children.

The Power of the Forgiven

When you are tempted to nurse a hurt and bear a grudge, you are tempted by a lie. The lie behind the temptation is that this grudge will restore some iota of your joy by granting you *power* over the person who has hurt you. Supposedly, you have the power to punish him by withholding your care and concern. You have the power to stop hurting because you've replaced the pain with anger.

Please don't buy the lie. Instead, understand the truth about forgiveness.

Some people view forgiveness simply as a state of affairs that settles down on a hurtful situation like a blanket, covering the evil and the pain. You were powerless when the sin occurred, and now you are powerless when the forgiveness happens. You resign yourself to say: "Well, okay, you get let off the hook *again,* and I'm the one who has to take it on the chin . . . *again."*

But forgiveness is really something we *do*—the powerful suds in the soap that wash away the pain instead of covering it. And because it is something we *do,* that means we are no longer powerless. Whatever others do to us—our husbands included—they can never take away the power we have to forgive them.

Jesus Christ placed himself into the hands of ruthless men. They used their power to strip him of his dignity. Eventually they took away his life. When Jesus hung on the cross, though he did it willingly, he was helpless. His hands were nailed to the rough wooden post as securely as his feet. Eventually, he began to lose the power to even push his body up so that he could breathe. But Jesus exercised the

Finding Freedom to Forgive

If you are still looking for freedom to forgive, read about the life of Joseph in Genesis 37–50.

If anyone had reason to bear a grudge, Joseph did. One moment he was the favored son of a wealthy shepherd, and the next moment he is a slave, sold into bondage in Egypt. His jealous brothers were going to kill him; instead they threw him into a pit and sold him to a caravan of Ishmaelites.

Even in Egypt, Joseph suffered offense. He was accused falsely by Potiphar's wife and thrown into prison. He was forgotten by the chief cupbearer, whom he had helped. The long days and nights in prison, I imagine, were a perfect time to nurse a grudge.

Later Joseph encounters his brothers again when he is amazingly the second-in-command of Egypt and they are begging for bread. Joseph had the legitimate authority; his brothers had committed a grievous crime; Joseph could have thrown them into prison for all they had done to him. But he didn't. He forgave.

What gave Joseph the freedom to forgive his brothers when I probably would have demanded they be thrown off the top of a pyramid?

Joseph had a perspective that you and I need to cultivate. He told his brothers, "And now do not be grieved or angry with yourselves, because you sold me here; for God sent me before you to preserve life. . . . It was not you who sent me here, but God" (45:5, 8). Later he told them, "And as for you, you meant evil against me, but God meant it for good in order to bring about this present result, to preserve many people alive" (50:20).

Did Joseph's brothers sell him into slavery? You bet they did. Are they responsible for their sin? Yes. But Joseph understood that God is a sovereign God who means to work good for his children. God is not a helpless sideline spectator who winces in sympathy when we get hurt. Instead, he is active and so sovereign that he can take the very sins of our husbands and produce good out of bad situations.

Imagine an assailant who comes toward you with a knife and stabs you in the belly. Is he guilty? Yes. Has evil resulted? Yes. But imagine a surgeon who does the same thing: inserts a knife or scalpel into your belly. He means it for good, and good results as a cancerous growth is removed. To make our analogy complete, though, imagine that this surgeon is so sovereign that he is actually able to use an assailant's attack to accomplish his own purposes. The assailant's knife goes in exactly the right place at exactly the right depth with exactly the right motion to remove the cancer. It's the one action (a knife in the belly) but accomplished simultaneously from an assailant who means it for evil (and is guilty) and a surgeon who means it for good (and is glorified).

Our God will make his enemies a footstool. He will use his enemies even to accomplish his good and kind purposes.

If your husband has hurt you, wait quietly on the Lord. The pain is real, but you will soon see that "the sufferings of this present time are not worthy to be compared with the glory that is to be revealed to us" (Romans 8:18). Trust God to work his surgeon's good.

Joseph did.

---

one power that the Roman legion could never take away from him. He exercised his power to forgive. "Father, forgive them, for they do not know what they are doing" (Luke 23:34, NIV).

Isn't that a minor victory, in light of the death that occurs? Or maybe one of those "moral victories" through which people try to recover some of their dignity? Hardly. In reality, forgiveness makes all the difference in the world. Not only is it a power that we exercise, but it is a power that empowers us even more. If Jesus hadn't risen from the dead, we might be tempted to say that his words of forgiveness merely add more poignancy to the tragedy: "Oh, look at how much he loved, even his enemies." Instead, we know that his forgiving, loving, sinless nature was the very thing that would prevent death from keeping him in the grave. Christ's words of forgiveness were part of his resurrection power. The Roman Empire has since crumbled, but Christ's kingdom is everlasting. Who had the greater power in the Crucifixion?

Our greatest "weapon" in the fight against the evil that invades our lives is to die to our wounded pride which demands revenge. We forgive, and in forgiveness we find supernatural power.

You may wonder why I've chosen to focus on the "power" aspect of forgiveness. The issue of power has dominated so much of the interaction between men and women, husbands and wives. As women, at some time we have all probably felt un-empowered, helpless in the face of a male-dominated society. Even in our homes, it's easy to feel helpless if we have a husband who rules with an overly authoritarian hand.

The whole language of the feminist movement is a language of power—who has it and who doesn't. While working on my master's degree in literature, I was exposed to the more militant form of feminism. Being a woman, I was automatically accepted as a potential collaborator, and I didn't face the heat of their anger (or maybe I sidestepped it). But I do remember standing in the hall after an exhausting day of exams. Plans were being made to go out for dinner, and one of the women stated that she would need to check with her husband first. This announcement was met with an outcry.

"Check with him?! *Tell* him what you're doing," one of the women commanded.

"Wait a minute," I countered. "Isn't this the very thing we don't want the men to do to us?"

"Exactly," was the reply. "We need to show them who's boss. I'd much rather be the one in charge."

In recent years, we've also seen the emergence of a "men's movement," spearheaded by such personalities as the poet Robert Bly or the Jungian psychologist Robert Moore. While I would be cautious to call it a supremacist movement, Bly's group does bemoan the powerlessness found in many men:

> Sometimes even today when I look out at an audience, perhaps half the young males are what I'd call soft. They're lovely, valuable people—I like them. . . . There's a gentle attitude toward life in their whole being and style of living. . . . You quickly notice the lack of energy in them. They are life-preserving but not exactly life-giving. Ironically, you often see these men with strong women who positively radiate energy.[1]

We've got two movements, both intent on carving out power for themselves. But something even greater is at work. Ken Canfield writes,

> With the militant feminist movement and much of the present men's movement, you actually see the inability of two movements to forgive each other. They both seek to be empowered by somehow stealing from the power base of the other, convinced that if one is strong, the other by necessity must be made weak. Christian men and women, however, can find *their* power from an outside source. And God's power is accessed by forgiving one another.

Let God's healing power enter your life as you forgive
your husband. When you forgive a wrong your husband has
committed against you, you begin the first steps of placing
that wrong behind you. You are no longer a slave to that incident; it no longer determines your thoughts, emotions, and
behavior. You have power to move on with your life.

True forgiveness empowers you to ward off bitterness. It
places a protective cloak around you and keeps bitterness
from taking root in your heart. I remember hearing an older
woman whom I loved and respected say, "I will never forgive
him for what he did to me." I don't know the details of the
offense, but I *do* know that he asked for her forgiveness. Yet
I saw her cold, unforgiving heart turn him away, refuse to
listen, refuse to understand. And I watched her destroy her
marriage, her family, and eventually herself. I watched as
the joy left her life and as she slowly sank into a bitter life of
self-destruction.

It does not need to be so. The ability to forgive quickly
and truly is a mark of spiritual maturity. It is evidence that
we are aware of God's grace, and willing to extend it to all
who need it.

Forgive one another: for the sake of your husband, for the
sake of your children, for your own sake. And because God,
who wants to give you the gift of a forgiving spirit and a forgiven home, commands it.

The Freedom to Forgive

How do we forgive when our husbands have intentionally
hurt us, when they have consistently disregarded our feelings and needs or those of our children? Let me repeat: Forgiveness does not mean that we condone the act. It does not
mean that we don't confront the wrongdoer. But if we are
Christians, forgiveness is not optional; it is mandated.

If we accept the two premises that (1) forgiveness can be difficult, but that (2) God nonetheless commands us to forgive, then we will want to pray this prayer: "Lord, create in me the freedom to forgive, and enable me to do that which is unnatural for me."

Even when we are hurt deeply by our husbands, hanging on to some important principles can help us forgive them.

Admit Your Own Inadequacies

Like your husband, you too sometimes make mistakes, sometimes sin, sometimes need forgiveness. When you can see yourself as just as sinful and fallen as your husband, you may find it easier to "do unto others what you would have them do unto you."

The most significant Person to extend us forgiveness is our Creator and Redeemer. When we compare ourselves to those around us we often have a tendency to feel quite righteous. We don't cheat on our taxes, we give to the poor, we are not filled with immoral thoughts, we live disciplined lives. Yet one cannot be immersed in Scripture and maintain a sense of self-righteousness. Can we possibly love as Christ loved? Are our hearts and minds continually filled with the awareness of his presence? Do we constantly live in obedience to that presence? Even the apostle Paul wrote, "For the good that I wish, I do not do; but I practice the very evil that I do not wish" (Romans 7:19). If Paul can say this, how much more can we, who are living in a society that is far removed from the memory of an incarnate Christ living among them?

Rejoice in the Fact that You Are Forgiven

Everyone who has stood with opened spiritual eyes at the foot of the cross has had to feel the overwhelming sense of awe at the love of our Savior: He was perfect, yet he died for sins that we, his creatures, have committed.

"There is therefore now no condemnation for those who are in Christ Jesus" (Romans 8:1). God has forgiven us of all those sins which resulted in the death of his innocent Son; as we meditate on his forgiveness, we find the freedom to forgive others.

Rejoice that You Are Not Asked to Do Something You Can't Do

The key to giving and receiving forgiveness is drawing on God's power. Admittedly, there are times when it is not *humanly* possible to bring ourselves to a place of forgiveness. This is when we are aware that there is a Power "who works in [us] to will and to act according to his good purpose" (Philippians 2:13, NIV). God does not command us to do something and then leave us alone to muddle through in our own strength. He has provided us with a Helper who enables us to do what we cannot possibly do on our own. The Spirit is able to open your eyes to see from your husband's perspective, to take away bitterness, and to grant forgiveness even when no one has asked for it.

Rely on God's Presence within You

It is one thing to know that God has promised to help you accomplish what he asks of you; it is another thing to claim this promise. Acknowledge God's presence in your life as the power that will enable you to see the need behind the guilt, to forgive, to put the past behind you, and to love.

Experience Hope

I have found that hope is one of the most crucial attributes I can possess in my marriage and in my family. If we truly believe that God is in control, that he is a good God, that "in all things God works for the good of those who love him, who have been called according to his purpose" (Romans 8:28, NIV), then we can go through tough times with a sense of hope. We can wake up seeing each day as full of potential for new and wonderful things. We can look at a relationship that seems to lack promise and be confident that God will work out his best purposes. Our focus is on the good God and not on the bad relationship.

Experience a Healthy or Healed Relationship With Your Own Father

The ability to encourage a husband through a forgiving spirit arises out of a processed and healthy relationship between a wife and her own father. If a wife has anger, resentment, fear, or anxiety remaining toward her own father, she will find it extremely difficult to stand aside, to trust, or to forgive her husband as he relates to her children. One of the greatest gifts she can give to her husband is a healthy or healed relationship with her father.

Forgiveness is a process, not a single act in time, and we must be willing to enter that process and continue in it as long as we have breath. We stand before God as women who need the help of whole, healthy, and effective fathers for our children. We realize all too well the difficulty of pulling the load ourselves. Our yokes grow heavy. Sometimes we have only accusations and condemnations for our husbands. Our complaints drone on and on.

God, give us the hearts to forgive . . . to see beyond the guilt and stand beside the need.

Questions for Personal Reflection

Think about these before discussion group.

1. You have probably been told by well-meaning friends at some time in your life when you have been hurt or offended, "You must forgive and forget." How does this comment make you feel when you find that you can't "forget"? Do you think it is *necessary* to forget in order to forgive?

2. Extending forgiveness in family reunions is hard to practice. How do you experience forgiveness in your family reunions? Think of your children as they grow older. How would you like to see them express and experience forgiveness in future family reunions?

3. What are some things that are easy to forgive in your husband?

4. What has been one of the most difficult things to forgive in your husband as it relates to your children?

Questions for Discussion

To discuss with a small group

1. Can you describe the feelings you had when you, as a condemned sinner, stood at the foot of the cross and felt the eyes of Jesus as he looked beyond all of the guilt that you knew was there and saw only your need? How can we share that same forgiveness with our husbands? Is it humanly possible?

2. Read Luke 23:34. Do you think anyone had asked for forgiveness? Why must we forgive, even when our forgiveness is not requested?

3. Which of the steps involved in forgiveness do you find most difficult?

4. How can your children benefit by seeing a mother who has a sincere forgiving heart?

The Driving Force

I have never heard of a yoked pair of oxen agreeing together to go plow a field or harvest a crop. I can't imagine any pair of oxen or horses that would have the ability to discern for themselves the jobs that need to be done, the task for which they were paired. Nor can we, as parents, assume that we can forge our own direction or that we have been left alone, abandoned to our own devices, cleverness, and training.

For several years when I was very young, my father worked a dairy farm which he had bought in New York state. A tractor came with the farm, but my dad mostly used his team of horses.

He had a special relationship with that team of horses. He felt proud of the way they called to him as he neared the barn in the early morning, and proud of the way they responded when he had them hitched up to the working gear. Those huge and powerful horses were able to trample or destroy anything that got in their way, yet they allowed my dad to put on the giant harnesses, hitch up the equipment behind them, and drive them into the fields day after day to work the crops and to bring in the harvests.

After he had them hitched up, they responded to his every command. A simple "Gee" or "Haw" would turn them right or left. Had they not been tuned in to his commands they would not have accomplished much at all; yet, with his

249

commands, my father made this pair of horses into a valuable and workable package. The three of them became the "team." With his knowledge and with their respect and affection for him they were also an *effective* team.

I find great comfort in the fact that Judd and I are not alone in this team effort of parenting. It is a tremendous task with eternal results. With all of our knowledge and experience there is still more to accomplish than our capabilities will allow.

And yet, our God holds the reins. As the faithful farmer, he has matched us for the task he has chosen for our particular team. Our responsibility is to be sensitive to the reins that are directing us, to stay in touch with the driver, to understand his heart, to trust his leadership and directions. God's part, according to his promise, is to lead us, to direct our paths.

> I will instruct thee and teach thee in the way which thou shalt go: I will guide thee with mine eye. (Psalm 32:8, KJV)
>
> And thine ears shall hear a word behind thee, saying, This is the way, walk ye in it, when ye turn to the right hand, and when ye turn to the left. (Isaiah 30:21, KJV)
>
> I lead in the way of righteousness, in the midst of the paths of judgment: that I may cause those that love me to inherit substance; and I will fill their treasures. (Proverbs 8:20-21, KJV)

Our reins are the Word of God, the still small voice that teaches us, the Spirit that gives us insight when we can't understand what in the world is going on around us. The reins are his discernment that is imparted through the Living Presence within us. The reins are our connection to the Great Eternal One, who sees the beginning from the end, whose purposes are indelibly written across the pages of time.

No, we are not dumb animals left to find our way, yoked together for nebulous purposes to be determined by fate alone. Yet so often we feel we are stumbling blindly along, powerlessly watching others hit the mark, and not understanding how or if we are going to make it at all as families.

Take courage! We have direction, we have protection, we have comfort; all are available just for the asking.

Five Appendixes

Mothers in Special Situations

The NATIONAL CENTER FOR FATHERING

A Fathers and Daughters

It may seem strange to think that a father can be confused by his daughters. After all, fathers have been raising daughters for almost as long as they have been on the earth. Nonetheless, we all know women who openly condemn their fathers for never really showing them the love they deserved. The truth is, we talk about "the battle of the sexes" and we laugh at jokes which point out the many differences between men and women in marriage, but too few of us realize that fathers face those same struggles in relating to their daughters.

Dale was a man's man, and would have been proud to be described as such. He loved football, hunting, and in certain moods, even all-star wrestling. Dale couldn't wait to be a father because, among other reasons, he wanted a son to take with him when he went hunting on Saturday mornings. He imagined the two of them tramping through the tall grass, his thick hand on the boy's shoulder, whispering to each other as they watched for the next covey of quail to be stirred into flight.

Unfortunately (or so Dale thought), God had chosen to bless him with three healthy, beautiful girls. And so Dale continued to go hunting with his friends and *their* sons, and eventually he grew to resent God for not giving him a son. As you would expect, Dale fathered his daughters almost from a distance. He didn't hate them, ignore them, or physically abuse them, but he almost purposely neglected to involve himself emotionally with them. How could girls measure up to his desire for a little rough-and-tumble version of himself?

Dale didn't demonstrate the deep affection and appreciation that his daughters so desperately wanted from him, and eventually the consequences surfaced. As his oldest daughter went through adolescence, she began to speak of her father as "a sick and selfish man," someone she had never really known and whom she had no desire to become close to. Eventually, as is so often the case, she sought the attention and approval that she didn't get from her father in an unhealthy relationship with another man.

Certainly, Dale is an extreme example. Most fathers don't consciously resent their daughters but *want* to honor them with affection and respect. Nevertheless, many well-meaning fathers find it very hard to relate to their young daughters, and the discomfort only gets worse as their daughters move into adolescence and experience the physical changes that come with it.

More and more experts are recognizing how fathers influence many aspects of a girl's progress into adulthood. In this short appendix, we want to identify several areas of a girl's life in which a father's absence or healthy involvement will have a profound effect. We present these not as weapons to use against an uninvolved father—which would only drive him further away—but as issues you can be aware of and encourage in your husband when you catch him doing them *right*.

A Daughter's Femininity and Sexuality

As a father notices his daughter's body beginning to bloom, his natural tendency is usually to shy away. She looks more like a woman now than the little girl she used to be. He hears the news about sexual abuse and incest in homes across the country, and just being around her makes him a little edgy. So, in his discomfort, he avoids any signs of affection that can be misconstrued in any way. Or, worse yet, he goes to the opposite extreme, and instead of saying nothing, he makes offhand remarks about her body and then laughs when she gets embarrassed.

What he doesn't realize is that this is the very time when a girl becomes extremely sensitive about the way her body is developing. There are *no* comments that are harmless; she will always wonder what her father *really* meant by what he said. It's very common for girls who have psychological eating disorders such as anorexia and bulimia to have fathers who tease them about their bodies.[1]

A girl watches her father as she forms her ideas about appropriate behavior between men and women. She's testing out her feminine charms in a safe environment, and it's a father's responsibility to show her what a proper, godly response sounds and feels like. A father *should* express to his daughter that she is beautiful in her new dress, or with her hair a certain way, but more importantly, he should express his love and respect for her as a person. If she learns at home that she is accepted and appreciated for her personal qualities, because of who she is, then she will be less likely to feel that she must earn love from men through physical means.

The early years of a father-daughter relationship have a great deal to do with whether or not an adolescent girl will become sexually active.[2] When a father honors his daughter for who she is, she will learn to expect the same honor in

[1] Nicky Marone, *How to Father a Successful Daughter* (New York: Fawcett Crest, 1988), 244.
[2] Donald E. Sloat, "Daughter's Dilemmas," *Church Herald* (Sept. 2, 1983):6

her future relationships with men. Richard Wesley, a writer in Los Angeles, put it this way:

> I am, as all fathers are, a daughter's "first boyfriend." That means that every man who comes into her life will be measured, for better or for worse, against me. And how a father treats his daughter—the lessons, both direct and indirect, that he has taught her—will determine her attitudes and behavior toward men. . . . If a man has cherished his daughter, she will probably choose men who will cherish her. . . . [He] must respect those unspoken boundaries of womanhood. Daughters must learn from their fathers that there are personal and sexual boundaries that no one—not even a father—has the right to cross.[3]

Another thing a father needs to communicate is that he has a healthy, God-given sexual relationship with his wife. He should promote a positive outlook about sexuality and make himself available to his daughter when she has questions about men's perceptions and thoughts about sex.[4] She will have questions, and she will find answers; a father can help to ensure that she learns *godly* answers.

A Daughter's Potential and Identity

What will a daughter do with her life, and how will she feel about it? While it's true that both parents have a great influence on the futures of their children, perhaps fathers affect their daughters most profoundly. Fathers are often a child's primary link to the outside world.

When a father sees his daughter venture out into new

[3] Richard Wesley, "My Daughters, My Heart," *Essence* (June 1992): 77.
[4] H. Norman Wright, *Always Daddy's Girl* (Ventura, Calif.: Regal Books, 1989), 274.

challenges, is he more likely to say, "What do you think you're doing?" or "Go for it; I'm proud of you"? Either message may spur her on to great achievement in whatever she pursues; the big difference will be in her motivations for success. She will either set high goals in order to prove her father wrong—in an almost obsessive chase for success—or she'll be confident of his love and encouragement no matter what she becomes. With her father's support, she'll be free to fail and learn through times of difficulty, but she'll also be inspired to do her best without always striving to win and achieve.[5] She finds her identity in being a child of a loving earthly and heavenly father, not in what she can achieve.

A Daughter's Emotions

Especially during the teen years, girls experience a whirlwind of emotions that change quickly and drastically. During this time, a father's natural tendency may be to lecture her about her unpredictable behavior, thinking it's just a phase she'll get through on her own. What she really wants is to be heard and understood, to sense that her feelings are important to her father, to know he's listening to her. Instead, his lectures prove that she's no match for him verbally or intellectually, and it becomes easy for her to want to strike back. Those girls whose fathers don't listen to them attentively can usually find ways to get through, even if it takes some drastic measure, like becoming pregnant.[6]

A Daughter's Ideas about Men

A father who is genuinely involved in the life of his daughter promotes a healthy view of men in general. Maybe some

[5] Ibid., 275.
[6] Sloat, "Dilemmas," 6.

men are chauvinistic, abusive, and/or irresponsible, but her father can be a lasting model of one very significant man who is consistent, trustworthy, and unafraid to show his emotions. She can be assured that, no matter what the latest psychobabble says, there *are* men out there who are warm and sensitive, but who can also direct their masculinity to keep their promises, overcome hardships, and endure the ups and downs that are inherent in relationships.

A Daughter's Ideas about Family

That little girl will grow up and, if she chooses, likely marry and have children of her own. As she and her husband begin to set up their own household, she will begin to remember things about her own father. Maybe it will be something about the way he hugged and talked to her after disciplining her; maybe the way he rewarded honesty in confrontations between family members. She will remember these things because her father led the family by laying out and enforcing rules, by making sure everyone was ready for church on Sundays, and by making their family outings so enjoyable. She has a vivid picture of what a healthy family looks like and how it functions, and she will peruse that mental picture many times as she becomes a parent herself and as she counsels other adults who are struggling in family relationships.

Practical Suggestions

What can you as a mother do to help your husband better relate to your daughters?

Help Your Husband Bridge the Biological Chasm
Men need extra help and insight when it comes to under-

standing and relating to daughters. With your help, your husband may have learned quite a lot about female behavior, but chances are he knows very little about what it's like to be a little girl. You do. Furthermore, as a mother, you see your children in situations and from perspectives that your husband cannot. You probably know much more about what your daughter is going through than he does, and so he must depend on you in order to understand her. Discussing these things is a major component in parenting any child, but it's especially important with daughters. The sooner he is able to understand her as a girl, the better.

Tell Him about Your Father

How did your father handle some of the issues raised in this appendix? Was he as affectionate as he could have been? Did he listen to you? How do you think it affected you?

Whether your memories of your father are positive or not, it may be more palatable for your husband to hear you talk about your own father than to have you tell him what to do (he'll call that nagging). If you had a strong, nurturant father, tell your husband about the security and confidence you gained from his attention. If your father had some shortcomings in relating to you as a daughter, this isn't an invitation to start father-bashing. But your husband may benefit from your pointing out some things you wish your father had done, and maybe describing the struggles you've encountered because of his inadequacies. Remember—the goal is insight for your husband.

Helpful Resources

Heather Harpham, *Daddy, Where Were You?* (Lynnwood, Wash.: Aglow Publications, 1991).

Nicky Marone, *How to Father a Successful Daughter* (New York: Fawcett Crest, 1988).

Maureen Rank, *Dealing with the Dad of Your Past* (Minneapolis, Minn: Bethany House, 1990).

H. Norman Wright, *Always Daddy's Girl* (Ventura, Calif: Regal Books, 1989). This book is directed more toward helping a woman understand her father's impact on who she is but also contains a chapter that gives tips for fathers of daughters.

B Fathers as Spiritual Leaders

One of the most common complaints among wives is that their husbands are not spiritual leaders in the household. Interestingly enough, among the thousands of fathers who make up our fathering data base, the vast majority of them see spiritual equipping of their children as one major area in which they would like to improve. A National Center for Fathering survey of pastors who are fathers found that *their* number one concern was becoming proficient at leading their children in spiritual matters. And as Ken travels around the country speaking to fathers, the question he is most commonly asked is, "What advice do you have for me about leading my family in devotions?"

In Deuteronomy 6:4-9 and numerous other places, the Bible clearly places the responsibility upon parents and, more specifically, upon fathers, to raise our children to "love the Lord your God." Tim Elmore, in his very helpful book *Soul Provider,* details four functions of an effective spiritual provider: a *model,* who tries to be a Christlike example; a *minister,* who humbly serves those around him; a *mentor,* who invests his life in others to encourage them and hold them accountable for their commitment to God; and a *manager,* who organizes and performs the functions of spiritual leadership.

The practical demonstrations of this leadership involve leading family devotions and prayer times, exposing children to godly influences, participating in their activities, and modeling personal disciplines himself.[1] As a wife, you have an important role in encouraging your husband in these activities. How does it make you feel when he prays with the kids before bed? Or when he reads from his Bible at breakfast? Tell him you appreciate him, and that he's making valuable investments in the lives of his children! Don't assume he's only doing what's expected of him, because these days, wives have learned to expect much less than that in the way of spiritual leadership.

A more common example would be the man who sat with his family there in our church for many years (there's probably one in your church, too). They took their place in their row, five or six of them, every Sunday. Their youngest child never caused a commotion, and the father never had to reach around to tap one of the kids on the shoulder and then scold him with a frown; he was never, never heard to whisper words of reproach to his kids in the middle of the sermon. They were so well behaved: They sang out during hymns, and they all bowed for prayers. From all appearances, there wasn't a more God-fearing family in the entire building.

And then, without warning, the father stopped coming. At first his wife said he was especially busy at work, but he didn't come for another month or so, and then another. Soon it was clear that he'd quit coming altogether, and eventually the children started dropping out, first the oldest, then the next, and so on. If Dad quit going to church, they figured, they could do their own thing just like him, and so the wife continued coming to church alone, usually bringing her

[1] Tim Elmore, *Soul Provider* (San Bernardino, Calif.: Here's Life Publishers, 1992), 43-46, 132-134.

young son with her. As the children grew, they continued to pursue "their own thing."

This woman faces the same question that many wives face when their husbands are not effective spiritual leaders: To what extent am *I* to assume the spiritual leadership which God intended for my husband?

We'd like to deal with this and other similar issues by addressing three different levels of a father's spiritual involvement.

Husbands Who Are Unbelievers

The verse we all think of in this situation comes from 1 Peter 3:1-4 (NIV):

> Wives, in the same way be submissive to your husbands so that, if any of them do not believe the word, they may be won over without words by the behavior of their wives, when they see the purity and reverence of your lives. Your beauty . . . should be that of your inner self, the unfading beauty of a gentle and quiet spirit, which is of great worth in God's sight.

Of course wives should take Peter's advice concerning unbelieving husbands, but you should also realize that you are still responsible to teach your children about a loving God who wants a personal relationship with each one of us. Your kids still need spiritual direction, and if your husband isn't providing it, then you need to step in. Chances are your kids are not getting spiritual direction at school.

God still commands you to be submissive to your husband as long as you are not disobeying God or putting yourself or your children in physical or emotional danger. Peter clearly understood that living with an unbelieving husband

puts a wife in a delicate—but very opportune—position. You
should still support and encourage him in his healthy fathering habits, and you should be very sensitive about your
words and actions. You must seek to please God first and
foremost, but also keep from offending or harassing your
husband by trying to force-feed him with spiritual truth.

In one way (though I'm *not* recommending it), having an
unbelieving husband can even be an advantage. Too many
women whose husbands *are* believers rely upon them
almost like priests, to the point where their relationship to
God is mediated almost entirely through their husbands. *No
matter what the situation, it is vital for every woman to cultivate her own spiritual walk with Christ.* If your husband is an
unbeliever, you may be more conscious of the need to take
the initiative for your own relationship to God—even though
your children will be more likely to take their faith strongly
to heart if their father is also involved in their spiritual training. You can pray that God will move powerfully to soften
the heart of your husband.

Believing Husbands Who Are Not Spiritual Leaders

Those of you in this situation may be the most frustrated of
all because, chances are, your husband knows that his children need spiritual training. You see so much untapped
potential for good in your husband that it's hard to understand why he isn't using it to benefit your children. Your husband's reasons for not following through could make up
another book entirely, but we do have a few suggestions on
how you can honor your husband and also honor God.

As Nancy describes in previous chapters, you should
remain supportive: You can believe in him and reinforce his
positive fathering practices both in private and in front of the

children; you can make your husband's spiritual leadership a regular subject in your personal prayers and also ask your close friends to lift him up to God. As always, you can continue to seek God daily as a part of your own spiritual growth and as you share your beliefs with your children.

If your husband is going to become a spiritual leader, you must do everything in your power to create an atmosphere of acceptance in the home. If he senses pressure to perform, the reluctance may grow even stronger. If he feels as though he's been given a script—written by you, with stage directions—and it's now his duty to play the part of spiritual leader, he'll obviously feel manipulated. If he's put in a leadership position he has not fully claimed (a kind of puppet-leader, if you will), his efforts will very likely be short-lived. Instead, a gentle and quiet spirit that communicates love and acceptance for who he is will be the most helpful approach.

Assuming your husband does attend church regularly, it is wise (for *any* wife!) to encourage him to develop friendships with other Christian men whom he admires. Men can say things to each other that wives cannot get away with, and you may be able to take advantage of the wisdom of other godly men who are spiritually engaged in the lives of their kids and who are concerned for your kids as well.

Husbands Who Are Trying to Be Spiritual Leaders

You're probably thinking, *If it's not broken, why fix it?* If your husband *is* doing his best to take on the spiritual leadership of the family, you have one more reason to thank God and praise your husband for being a committed father. Our thoughts in this section are directed toward wives who want to encourage their husbands to become even *more* effective spiritual leaders, who want to keep from *dis*couraging their husbands in any way.

Let's assume your husband is praying with his children, regularly leading in family devotions, and using everyday occurrences to point out the power and grace of God—but he just isn't very good at doing these things. What should you do? Continue to support him and pray for him, of course, and be even more sensitive to how you're reacting to his leadership.

Tim Elmore quoted one wife who said that "women really do hunger for men to be spiritual leaders. But because so few of them know how, we tend to take control of the relationship. Eventually, though, we do it out of resentment."[2] It may be a natural tendency for you to want things done *right* (by your standard), and in your admirable desire to want what's best for your children, you may trample your husband's feelings. As the words of this woman demonstrate, when wives "take control," it naturally causes resentment in both partners.

But short of taking control, it can also discourage your husband if you give him running critiques of his spiritual guidance, or if you constantly offer suggestions for his improvement. If you embarrass him in front of the kids, expect him to be reluctant to try his hand at it again very soon. He will be more encouraged if he feels the two of you are working as a team (driven by his leadership).

A husband will sense a huge difference between a wife who is proud of his efforts—though they may be feeble—and a wife who measures him against a high set of expectations. Maybe you're used to Charles Swindoll's preaching on the radio or James Dobson's timely advice; maybe the pastor

[2] Ibid., 16.

at your church is especially understanding; maybe another man in Sunday school always seems to say the right things when he prays; maybe the youth minister really knows how to get your kids fired up for the Lord. These are all blessings from God, but what father can stand up to such expectations and still be motivated to confidently lead his family? If your husband is given time and an atmosphere of acceptance, if he is allowed to fail, and learn, and keep trying to serve his family in a spiritual way, God may do things through him that you never would have dreamed were possible.

It is God's design for your husband to learn to use his unique spiritual gifts creatively as he works out his own style of leadership. And, if he is receptive to what God wants for his children, he will recognize and utilize the natural spiritual intimacy and insights that you as a mother bring to the family.

Helpful Resources
Elizabeth Baker, *Wanting to Follow, Forced to Lead* (Wheaton, Ill.: Tyndale House Publishers, 1991).

Tim Elmore, *Soul Provider* (San Bernardino, Calif.: Here's Life, 1992).

Ann Gimenez, *The Emerging Christian Woman* (Altamonte Springs, Fla.: Creation House, 1986).

C Hope for Single Mothers

One of the greatest threats to the American family today—yes, even in the Christian community—is divorce. If your life has been touched by this tragedy, you know it all too well: the whole painful process that starts with surprise, shifts into shock, resentment, depression, and hostility, and moves through a whole range of inexpressible emotions which linger for years, if not for the rest of your life.

Those who haven't been through it can never understand it completely, and you're probably not sure you understand it all yourself. There are too many complex feelings to sort out without piling on all the other day-to-day deadlines you have to meet just to survive.

Since the number of divorced mothers who receive custody of their children is somewhere between 80 and 90 percent,[1] we assume that you (or someone you know) are among that group. The frustration of the entire divorce process has left you exhausted physically, financially, emotionally, and spiritually. You look back at your marriage and feel violated, perhaps even abused.

But then you think of the children, and that opens up a whole new range of emotions. They are so precious, and yet there may be so much tension between you and them. They don't understand your pain from the breakup; they're too

[1] Paul L. Adams, Judith R. Milner, and Nancy A Schrepf, *Fatherless Children* (New York: John Wiley & Sons, 1984), 27.

busy with their own emotions. No matter how much you tell
them you love them, they can't help but feel somewhat abandoned by one or both of their parents. And the situation
worsens when they've been pulled back and forth or used by
their father to get back at you, like human weapons on an
emotional battleground.

But simply bringing up the painful emotions of divorce
does nothing to combat the immediate problem—we confess that it's so much easier to write an appendix about it
than it is to gear up for the daily struggle of single parenting.
That struggle becomes even more trying when your ex-husband, the man who years ago pledged to love you faithfully
and unceasingly, seems to be doing everything in his power
to make your life more complicated, more burdensome.

There is hope for all divorced parents in the knowledge
that it *will* get easier in time. You may never have the perfect, blissful family that is often conjured up in the minds of
so many evangelical Christians, but by God's grace there is
healing, there is promise for a fulfilling future for you and
your children.

Tensions after the Divorce

After a divorce, there is typically a two-year cycle of conflicting tensions which devastates many mothers. Depending on
the specific situation, the number of children you have and
their ages, this cycle can take as long as five years to run its
course. But be encouraged; things will get better. Christian
mothers can take full assurance that these difficult times
develop the kind of perseverance spoken of in James 1,
which brings "the crown of life that God has promised to
those who love him" (v. 12, NIV).

The time immediately after the divorce brings a flood of

self-doubt and disillusionment at the realization that your marriage has failed, the vows have been broken. As if you would forget otherwise, you are constantly reminded of this fact by insensitive "friends," negotiations for custody, child support and visitation, and the adjustments to a new way of relating to your former husband. At the outset, your children will probably be relieved that the days of living in anxiety are over. Depending on their ages, they may not understand your distress, and may even seem to be coping as if everything was just fine.

About a year after the divorce, you will feel as though you have made the necessary adjustments to your new status, and may even be settling in comfortably—though single parenting is never easy. But this is usually the time when children experience the most difficulty in dealing with the divorce. They are being transported back and forth between parents, possibly flying long distances by themselves, and trying to deal with their feelings about the separate and sometimes conflicting relationships with their mom and dad. The reality of their divided family has sunk in, bringing all its confusion, and bringing back more shock waves for you, their mother. Some divorced mothers have described their relationship with their children at this time to be "declared war," "a struggle for survival," "the old Chinese water torture," or "like getting bitten to death by ducks."[2]

As the two-year mark approaches, you have helped your children learn to cope with their new situation, but now a new ordeal is just reaching its peak in your life. You have given two years of effort and attention to reestablishing some semblance of normalcy at home, and now the thought

[2] E. M. Hetherington, M. Cox, and R. Cox, "The Aftermath of Divorce," in *Mother-Child, Father-Child Relations,* ed. J. H. Stevens, Jr., and M. Mathews, (Washington, D.C.: National Association for the Education of Young Children, 1978), 163, 170.

of venturing out into the community again seems over-whelming. You're becoming more and more aware of your plight as a divorced mother: trying to adjust socially to being alone; realizing that if your kids are still very young, they'll need up to fifteen more years of your dedicated attention; feeling the tremendous responsibility you alone have to guide them through the many temptations as they grow up; and feeling the lack of resources and services available to help single mothers survive it all.

Easing the Tension

We have six suggestions which we believe will help you and your children alleviate some of the friction and make the best of a difficult situation:

Maintain Healthy Communication with Your Children
One of the biggest challenges is to consider the needs of your children while still taking care of yourself. They need to express and work through their emotions about what has happened, so you need to consistently ask them about their feelings. Encouraging them to express themselves will also keep the lines of communication open, which will help smooth the process for all concerned. Your children can become encouraging partners through the adjustment process, or they can seem like your worst enemies. By establishing open communication with them from the beginning, you will set up a positive method for coping with conflict that will spill over into other situations you'll face as a family.

Present a Healthy Home Atmosphere
Though single mothers are one of the most neglected groups in our society today, we know you don't want to use

that as an excuse for not being accountable to God for how you raise your children. You may feel overwhelmed at times, but don't let their father's absence defeat you. You can give your children the security they need by keeping a regular, predictable schedule. Your household can still be balanced with love and discipline.

One thing that will help you tremendously is to maintain connections to healthy families in your church or circle of friends. Making an effort in this area should be a priority. You are doing your best, but you need to give your children regular exposure to at least one other household where the husband and wife show love for each other and work together to build confident, well-adjusted children. Being connected to such people will create an atmosphere of mutual acceptance and accountability, and demonstrate positive family interaction for you and your kids. Children of divorced parents statistically tend to end up divorced themselves; but this is less likely to happen if your children have seen up close how healthy marriages operate. One of your greatest gifts to your children can be exposing them to healthy, intact families.

Identify Healthy Male Role Models
Your children have important needs that can be met only by men. This entire book is based upon the truth that children glean something valuable from the masculine perspective that they cannot get from their mothers. Furthermore, all children need *someone* they see regularly who models healthy, Christian male behavior. If your children's father is not in a situation to provide this, it is up to you to seek men who can and will. This is especially true for sons, who need to be "called out" into the world of masculinity, although

daughters also need the positive influence of a man (see our
appendix on fathers and daughters).[3]

The man may be the child's uncle, coach, teacher, or
someone in your church. But once you have found a male
mentor whom you trust, many of the principles for encouraging fathers—and keeping from hindering them—can be
applied as you encourage this man's interaction with your
children. You can pray regularly for him, accept him and his
uniquely male way of interacting with the children, and give
him feedback.

Seek Out a Support System for Yourself and *for Your Children*
Kari is a divorced mother with a four-year-old daughter. She
had been attending a church for over seven years, since
before she was married, and had many good friends there.
But in the years following her divorce, she began to feel that
her needs weren't being met, that she no longer belonged
among those she still knew so well. Several months later she
began attending another church, a smaller fellowship where
she made new friends and received more support from
those around her.

We're not suggesting that you change churches for Kari's
reasons but, like Kari, you *do* need to find a support system
made up of willing, reliable people. Maybe it will be a professional counselor instead of a church group. Whatever the
case, a broader community of supporters can give you the
help you will need from time to time. Just as important, a
support group can also be a sounding board for the way you
are raising your kids, and provide you with another perspective on what is going on in their lives. At the end of the day,
when you're especially vulnerable to outbursts of anger,

[3] Gordon Dalbey, *Healing the Masculine Soul* (Dallas: Word, 1988), 35-58.

you'll be more likely to check a negative reaction toward your children if you know someone will be calling you later to ask how things are going.

You mustn't expect people in your church to approach you, hand you their phone number, and say, "I'm here for you, and I'm praying for you. Call me anytime, day or night." It may happen (praise God if it does!), but the truth is there are too few churches who are truly meeting the needs of single mothers. Instead of waiting for others to approach you, *you* will have to assess your own needs as a single mother, ask God to guide you, and then *seek out* a number of people and make specific requests—prayer, baby-sitting, finances, 24-hour "hotline" accessibility, etc. Provide people with the opportunity to help you without placing expectations on them, and let God answer your prayers and meet your needs through whomever he chooses.

Seek God in Prayer

It's so easy to question the sovereignty of God in the midst of the turmoil of divorce, and it's easy to resent God for years afterward. But however sore and numerous your emotional scars may be, true healing can come only through reconciliation to God through Jesus Christ. If you work through the pain and turmoil with the Lord, your children will be more likely to follow your example. You need to ask specifically for his healing for yourself and for your children. He may not magically take away your pain, but he has promised to be with you through everything and help you gain the strength to persevere. Since your children have no father to guide their spiritual development on a daily basis, ask God to empower you as you lead your children to the *true* Father who never abandons his children.

Adopt a Positive Attitude toward Your Children's Father
We have saved this one for last because it may be the toughest for you to swallow. However, it is also one of the most essential suggestions in this entire appendix. Divorce naturally produces resentment and bitterness between a man and woman, but even though he is no longer your legal husband, *he is still your children's father.* Unless you have reason to suspect physical, emotional, or sexual abuse, a civil relationship between divorced parents will minimize the confusion and insecurity in the children.

To take this a step further, encourage your ex-husband as a father to your children. Give him space; encourage him to be involved. Do everything you can to support him in his fathering. For example, give him feedback: If his times with the kids have become "blowout weekends" filled with amusement parks, baseball games, and Pizza Hut, explain to him how hard life is when they come back home to early bedtimes and tuna sandwiches. Tell him they want *him,* not gifts and roller coasters. Most of the principles in the previous chapters can still be applied with positive results.

May we even suggest that you can pray for him as a father? Even if you look at your husband as an enemy, doesn't Jesus command us to pray for our enemies (Matthew 5:44)? When you pray for someone, you can't help but desire the best for him. And if your attitude toward him is softened to any degree, if you become the least bit more inclined to see yourself as part of a parenting team, if your children hear you speak about him with more respect than resentment, more warmth than rage, you're giving them that much more of a secure base as they move out into the world on their own.

We at the National Center for Fathering believe in marriage, but we also believe God has mercy on those who suffer. In a world where divorce continues to bring suffering to millions every year, God promises to be "a father to the fatherless, a defender of widows" (Psalm 68:5, NIV). We pray that his people will rise up and become the instruments of God's grace toward divorced mothers and their children.

Helpful Resources

Robert G. Barnes, Jr., *Single Parenting* (Wheaton, Ill.: Tyndale House Publishers, 1984)

Larry Burkett, *The Complete Financial Guide for Single Parents* (Wheaton, Ill.: Victor Books, 1991)

Andy Bustanoby, *Single Parenting* (Grand Rapids, Mich.: Zondervan, 1992)

Dandi Daley Knorr, *Just One of Me* (Wheaton, Ill.: Harold Shaw Publishers, 1989)

Alice Stolper Peppler, *Single Again—This Time With Children* (Minneapolis, Minn.: Augsburg, 1991)

D Stepfathers

Stepfathers make up the most rapidly emerging group of fathers in our nation. Recent estimates have placed the number of divorced mothers who remarry at around 80 percent. Every new stepfather walks into an emotional mine field as he tries to simultaneously recover from the wounds in his own past, build a new marriage with you as his wife, and settle into this new family situation with your children and possibly children from a previous marriage. And all this takes place in the aftermath of your ex-husband, whose presence still seems to linger mystically—if not physically—in the shadows of this new household. It isn't surprising that a large percentage of abuse cases occur in step-families or mixed families.

But there are stepfathers who are truly God's instruments of hope and healing to fatherless homes, and these men deserve our praise for their willingness to step in and be a father figure for those who have none. They will also need your grace and encouragement, because they face a tremendous challenge.

Perhaps the greatest point of tension for a new stepfather is knowing how and to what extent he should be involved in the discipline of your children. Here are two examples that illustrate right and wrong ways of handling this issue:

Janice married Reggie because they needed each other. Both of them had problems from their previous marriages, and they decided they could help each other heal. Reggie believed strict discipline is God-ordained, and so naturally he began to take control with Janice's kids, and Janice felt it was right to yield completely to his authority. But Reggie placed on her children expectations for which she had never prepared them, and instead of protecting her children from his heavy-handed discipline and criticism, she gave him full authority over them. He took it upon himself to make them conform to his own views regarding their music and many of their other habits—things she had never really worried about in the past.

As you would expect, the children didn't take to Reggie very well. The family entered counseling not long after he moved in; one son became a delinquent, and one of Janice's daughters underwent psychiatric care and was eventually placed in another home. This family demonstrates the major and lasting fallout when a stepfather dives in or is pushed into a role as disciplinarian with his new children.

Norm and Trudy are a far different story. After Trudy filed for divorce because of her ex-husband's homosexual tendencies, she and her kids were utterly disillusioned. When Norm, who had never been married, met Trudy and they began to think about marriage, their plans included her four children. They discussed his role in discipline—he would be there to back up Trudy and support her decisions, and if he had any questions or disagreements he would bring them up in private, away from the kids.

This kind of sensitivity on Norm's part not only won him a loving wife, but her kids also viewed him as an answer to their prayers. His devotion to Trudy has strengthened their marriage and her children's sense of security. Men like Norm should give us all hope in knowing that God can provide children with the male leaders that they need.

Another challenge every stepfather faces is to remember that his primary responsibility is to love you, his wife. The two of you may be able to build a marriage that's as strong as any other, but as a stepfather, he can never truly be a *father* to your children. This presents him with some real disadvantages, but also gives him certain advantages. He doesn't have blood connections to your children, so there won't be the natural emotional attachment, but the pressure and expectations that real fathers face won't be there either. He may have more difficulty establishing close relationships with your children, but whatever he does accomplish with them will be a bonus instead of a half-fulfilled obligation.

A stepfather is really more like a mentor than a father. He's a helper, a caretaker, a *steward* of sorts, who gives your children a needed perspective and becomes an important source of strength as they grow and mature. He doesn't actually have the responsibility that you do in raising them—though he can earn that responsibility over time—but he does possess a potential to influence them which is equal to, though different than, yours. Your encouragement can be a major factor in equipping him to be a blessing to your kids.

Let us suggest five ways in which a mother can ease the tension in her husband's stepfathering:

Don't Force Your Children to Call Him "Dad"
Your marrying another man has brought your children some new and not entirely welcome obligations and commitments *that they have not chosen to make*. Forcing them to accept your husband on your terms will only cause resentment, especially with older kids as opposed to very young children, who may accept and love him almost immediately. But you must allow your children to define their own comfort zones as they relate to their stepfather. It's

natural to want your family to adjust as quickly as possible, but that desire will be best served by patiently allowing your husband to earn the respect and love of your children in *their* time.

Keep Encouraging your Children's Relationship with Their Biological Father

What often happens when a divorced mother remarries is that everyone in the household tries to forget the ex-husband completely. This new family has a good chance of working, you say, and you don't need to stir up memories and bring back all the tears. But no matter how hard you try, you can't forget your children's father, and neither can your children. If you attempt to ignore his existence, trying to keep his bones in the closet, so to speak, you can be sure that sooner or later, probably during a confrontation, your children will not only drag those bones out, but will even use them as weapons against you.

The better alternative is to be open and honest about your ex-husband in your household. If he continues to try to be involved with his kids, encourage him in that, remembering that *he* is their father—not your present husband—and that your children have a need to be reconciled to him, to feel at peace about their relationship to him. Your new husband may grow to have a lasting and rewarding relationship with your children, but setting him up as the "new father" and asking them to accept him as a replacement to their real father is only asking for turbulence in the future, if not right away.

Schedule Regular Times Away from the Kids as a Couple

Even more than in first marriages, it is vital that you and your husband spend time alone, strengthening and revitalizing your marriage. Besides the benefits you will see as a couple, your children will take great comfort in your commitment to one another. They've already seen one marriage end, and many children even blame themselves for it. Their outlook on life each day will greatly improve if they sense love and commitment between their mother and stepfather at home.

These outings can also serve as times of reassessment and planning as you work to encourage your husband's relationships with your children. If all wives are ambassadors of sorts between fathers and their children, they are even more essential to stepfathers. You are really the key person in the situation. You know your new husband well, and you know your kids. You also know your children's father: his influence, and his strengths and weaknesses. Time away with your husband can be a wonderful opportunity to ask how you can encourage and help him as he relates to your children, to give him thoughtful feedback on his efforts, and to help him interpret your kids' behavior.

Give Him Your Acceptance

You thought it was tough in your first marriage. The prince moved in and brought with him all his annoying, sloppy, froglike habits. But now there are two or three or four of you who have to adjust to this new man's peculiarities, and when it's three on one you may find it easy to join in the laughter or criticism. But think about what those little comments and giggles do to your husband. He may not get mad, or talk back, but you are in effect separating him as a kind of outsider from the rest of the family—not the ideal position for someone you want to help raise your kids.

He is depending on your help as he settles into your family, and his best efforts to relate positively to your kids will come out of a feeling of confidence and acceptance, not alienation. Your flexibility toward his manners and personal habits will provide a model for your children as they learn to accept him into the family as he is, faults and all. And you will demonstrate the kind of adaptable spirit he will need as *he* learns to deal with the idiosyncrasies of your kids and your family atmosphere.

Discuss Discipline and Exercise It with Extreme Caution
We felt this point was important enough to warrant this short reminder.

Helpful Resources

David and Bonnie Juroe, *Successful Stepparenting* (Old Tappan, N.J.: Revell, 1983)

Dr. Larry Richards, *Remarriage: A Healing Gift from God* (Dallas: Word, 1981)

Dr. Dwight Small, *Remarriage and God's Renewing Grace* (Grand Rapids, Mich.: Baker, 1986)

Jim Smoke, *Growing in Remarriage* (Old Tappan, N.J.: Revell, 1990)

Judson J. Swihart and Steven L. Brigham, *Helping Children of Divorce* (Downer's Grove, Ill.: InterVarsity Press, 1982)

E Abusive Fathers

A quick scan of some of the synonyms listed for "abusive" helps to describe some of the emotions an abused child must experience: belittling, derogatory, disparaging, insulting, slanderous, brutal, cruel, harsh, foul, obscene, offensive. And if these words stir up strong emotions in our imaginations, those who have experienced it know that the reality of abuse is even worse.

Every day someone new admits he or she was abused as a child, and everyone always mentions that they still suffer from it even today, as an adult. Recently Ken was on the phone with a friend of his, a prominent speaker in the Christian community, who was having marital problems. This man has often described how he could never live up to his father's expectations, and how he was constantly belittled as he grew up. When Ken offered to call a renowned Christian author and counselor who might take the time to help this couple, the man fell silent. After a moment, he said, "Oh, he wouldn't talk to me. I'm nothing compared to him." This man with grown children himself still feels unworthy of that counselor's time, even though his father's abuse happened so many years ago.

Even with the increased awareness of child abuse in our society, too many women are still blind to it when it happens in their own household. There's nothing more tragic than someone who is witnessing abuse without even knowing it. Granted, this whole issue can be confusing; some people in our society believe parents shouldn't do *anything* that causes their child to be unhappy, not to mention spanking or other forms of discipline.

Where do you draw the line; when is behavior abusive?

We're not going to talk about numbers of swats or how long a child should be made to sit in his room; it's never that simple. Instead, here's what may be a new way of looking at it. Many people think of abuse as discipline that's carried too far, where the child is being physically injured. That *is* abuse in many cases, but a better way of looking at it may be to consider the *emotional atmosphere* of the interaction between parent and child. Look again at the synonyms for "abuse": cruel, insulting, belittling, harsh. . . . Many of these words can be applied to physical acts, spoken words, or even gestures. A parent can physically discipline a child to discourage wrong behavior while still affirming the child as a person, or a parent can be abusive in speaking three or four words, or even in a condemning stare. Everything depends on the emotion the parent communicates.

Rather than thinking of abuse as crossing a line on a progression of parental behavior, it should be viewed in terms of the parent's *motives* behind the behavior. Abuse is *not* ordinary discipline that is taken too far; it's something entirely separate from healthy discipline, borne out of a completely different mind-set. Is the parent looking after the child's best interests, or is he or she simply exploding at the end of a frustrating day, and the child just happened to be in the wrong place at the wrong time? Is the child corrected for his own good, or is he humiliated for something that really wasn't that bad?

There was a family in a small farming community in which the father believed he should cuss out and beat up his boys to keep them from being arrogant. His wife watched her sons being humiliated in front of the family for years, and she didn't really think anything was wrong with it until one of her sons got married and had a child of his own. One day she heard that he'd been put in jail for child abuse, and that her eighteen-month-old granddaughter was in the hospital with a skull fracture and several broken ribs. Her son had beaten his baby daughter for soiling her pants, leaving her physically handicapped for life. The son was sent to the state penitentiary and his wife later divorced him, and his mother was left to remember the abuse she had allowed to continue in her household for years.

This story illustrates several important ingredients of child abuse from which all mothers can learn. First, too many wives do not stand up to their abusive husbands; instead, they enable the abuse to continue. In most families it is the father's role to be the protector, but when he becomes a threat instead of a source of security, it is the wife's duty to recognize the abuse and take action to protect her children. By doing nothing, a wife essentially acts as a perpetrator of the abuse. Her efforts to be a nurturing mother will be negated, her children will doubt her love as well as their father's, and the cycle of abuse will only grow worse as her kids grow up and have children of their own.

Second, most abusive fathers were abused themselves, and their natural tendency is to carry on that legacy of pain. If your husband was abused as a child, you play an important role in helping him deal with his own past and break the cycle of abuse which has been passed down to him. He probably wouldn't think of his father's treatment as abuse, or of himself as a potential or acting abuser, but with your help he can begin to understand what forces are acting upon him as a husband and father. Talk to him about his past as it relates to his father's discipline and verbal interactions. If you can help him access his feelings about his own abuse, the chances are good that he'll gain valuable insight into his attitudes and behavior toward his own children.

Substance Abuse

There are other problems commonly tied to child or spouse abuse which fall under the category of substance abuse. Very often the substance abuse is the root cause of the other abuse, and it brings to your family a whole new range of problems. If your husband has difficulty controlling his temper when he's clear-headed, he may be even more dangerous to your children when his thought processes have been influenced by alcohol or drugs.

Too many wives become enablers of their husband's behavior by trying to cover for him. They call in sick for him when he's actually hung over; they make excuses to cancel engagements when he's in no shape to be seen in public; and, what is possibly most harmful, they make excuses for him in front of the children. It's true that the children may have difficulty understanding why their father behaves like he does, but they will be much worse off if their mother lies to them to protect them from the truth. Again, this topic deserves much more attention than we can give it here, but if you feel that your husband may have a problem with substance abuse, it's critical that you seek outside help before he does irreparable damage to your family. There are support organizations in most cities (such as Al-Anon for wives, and Alateen for children of alcoholics) which have helped to restore hope in many suffering families.

Recognizing Abuse

Abuse can be physical, emotional, sexual, or any combination of the three. In an effort to keep from overwhelming you, we're providing only some of the most common indicators that your child is being abused:

- unexplained bruises, welts, or burns
- unexplained fractures, lacerations, or abrasions
- extreme wariness of adult contact
- extremely aggressive or withdrawn behavior
- abnormally vacant or frozen stares
- unattended physical problems or medical needs
- reports from professionals of lagging physical or emotional development
- bizarre, sophisticated, or unusual sexual gestures or behavior[1]

Steps to Take When Abuse Is Suspected

Recognize the Situation

What is your husband's attitude toward you and the children? Does he make threats? Does he often make the family fearful and on edge, or does he carry out his fathering duties in an atmosphere of love? Take a good look at how he behaves, not only toward your children, but also toward *you*. Most cases of child abuse also involve abuse of the mother, which may make confronting him that much more difficult. But if he abuses you as well, that makes it all the more imperative that you do seek help. If you let it go on, thinking he'll get over his temper, most likely he'll only get worse.

Take Refuge in a Safe Environment If Necessary

We don't want to promote an alarmist attitude concerning your husband's behavior toward your children, but it *is* vital that you take action appropriate to the danger in

[1] Adapted from J. Louer, I. Lourie, M. Salus, and D. Broadhurst, *The Role of the Mental Health Professional in the Prevention and Treatment of Child Maltreatment* (Washington, USDHEW, 1980).

which you and your children are living. If you and/or your
children have become immobilized with fear, if the normal, healthy activities of your household have been dis-
rupted because of your husband's tyrannical whims or
threatening remarks, something must be done. If he
knows he can get away with anything he wants, he probably won't see any reason to change; but if he knows you
are prepared *and willing* to do what's necessary to protect
yourself and your children, chances are he will think more
about the impact of his words and actions.

Maybe it will be enough to take your children to a friend's
house for the evening to give your husband time to calm
down, or maybe the situation will be dangerous enough that
you'll need to call the police. There's no guaranteed formula;
this is where your discernment becomes important. Be sensitive to how your children's feelings are affected by your
husband and, when necessary, take action that is *appropriate* to the danger.

Seek Outside Help

In many ways, every household is its own little system,
where everyone plays a part and everyone understands how
things are run. Your children can learn to justify your husband's abusive behavior just as easily as you can. You love
him, after all; he just loses control once in a while. If you *do*
suspect your husband's behavior is perhaps a little severe, if
there's a small voice inside which keeps whispering, "This
doesn't feel right," you should listen to it.

Bring a trusted friend, your pastor, or a counselor into the
situation. Open up this closed system and allow someone
from the outside to help you assess what is happening. This
person will have an objective, uninvolved perspective and can
help you decide just how dangerous your husband's behavior

is. If you're convinced that something does need to be done, this person will be your support as you confront your husband and seek to help him learn new habits in the home.

Recruit People to Hold Your Entire Family Accountable

Once the problem has been identified and confronted and your husband has acknowledged the problem, you will need concerned Christian friends who regularly check in on you to monitor your family's recovery process. During counseling or whatever help you choose, there can always be relapses into destructive behavior, or your children may still be bitter toward their father. Your support team will be available if you need a sounding board, baby-sitters, someone to pray with, etc.

Establish New Patterns

Your marriage and home life can move on through the healing power of forgiveness, but it will involve more than just putting the past behind; it will require you to begin assuming the best of your husband and encouraging him in positive fathering habits. It will probably still be a struggle for him, but it will boost his confidence to know that you are working on his behalf, that you are an understanding partner.

Perhaps this process will be better illustrated by Carla and her husband, Patrick. Carla was concerned about the way Patrick disciplined their daughter. He liked to make her sit in the corner for what Carla thought was too long, and his physical discipline went further than it needed to. She finally mentioned it to a friend, and the friend suggested that it did sound like it was a problem and she should trust her instincts.

Carla confronted Patrick about it, and he became angry, told her she was crazy, and stormed out of the room. She went to her pastor, and he arranged a meeting with them, and he also invited several church elders and a counselor. Patrick felt embarrassed and ganged up on at first, but he grudgingly accepted the advice to attend counseling. The church elders continued to call on Patrick and Carla regularly, and the counselor learned that Patrick himself had been abused as a child.

It has taken a long time for Patrick to feel comfortable in his parenting again, but whenever he feels the old extreme tendencies coming on as he relates to his daughter, he has learned to call Carla and together they decide on the best course of action. By taking action when she was convinced there was abuse, Carla has given her marriage a new sense of hope and has saved her children and grandchildren from the pain of the ongoing cycle of abuse.

Helpful Resources

James Alsdurf and Phillis Alsdurf, *Battered into Submission* (Downer's Grove, Ill.: InterVarsity Press, 1989)

Claudia Black, Ph.D., M.S.W., *It Will Never Happen to Me!* (Denver: M.A.C. Printing, 1981)

Claudia Black, Ph.D., M.S.W., *Repeat after Me* (Denver: M.A.C. Printing, 1985)

Lynda D. Elliott and Vicki L. Tanner, Ph.D., *My Father's Child* (Brentwood, Tenn.: Wolgemuth & Hyatt, 1991)

Jan Frank, *A Door of Hope* (San Bernardino, Calif.: Here's Life Publishers, 1987)

Lynn Heitritter and Jeanette Vought, *Healing Victims of Sexual Abuse* (Minneapolis, Minn.: Bethany House, 1989)

Karen Burton Mains, *Abuse in the Family* (Elgin, Ill.: David C. Cook, 1987)

Notes

Chapter 1

1. Elisabeth Elliot, "The Essence of Femininity: A Personal Perspective." Paper presented at the Congress of Biblical Manhood and Womanhood, 1989.
2. Sara McLanahan and Karen Booth, "Mother-Only Families: Problems, Prospects, and Politics," *Journal of Marriage and the Family* 51 (1989): 557–80.

Chapter 2

1. Diane M. Byrne, "Dads Help Preemies Develop," *Healthy Kids Birth* 3 (Spring/Summer 1991): 10.
2. Lee Horton, "The Father's Role in Behavioral Parent Training: A Review," *Journal of Clinical Child Psychology* 13 (1984): 274–79.
3. Ross D. Parke, *Fathers* (Cambridge: Harvard University Press, 1981), 86.

Chapter 3

1. Stephen Covey, *The Seven Habits of Highly Effective People* (New York: Simon and Schuster, 1989), 238–39.
2. Ibid., 241.
3. A. Calhoun, *A Social History of the American Family,* vol. 1 (New York: Barnes and Noble, 1945), 115.
4. Paul Leavitt, "Single-Parent Families on Rise," *USA Today* (Sept. 15, 1992): 3A.
5. Julia Lawlor, "Men Seeking More Family Time Fear 'Wimp Factor,'" *USA Today* (June 14, 1991): B1.

6. Jack Balswick, *Why I Can't Say I Love You* (Waco, Tex.:
   Word, 1978), 34.

Chapter 4

1. Armand M. Nicholi and George Rekers, eds., *Family
   Building* (Ventura, Calif.: Regal Books, 1985), 52.
2. U.S. Census Bureau, quoted in Leslie Baldacci, "Dad's
   Absence Takes Heavy Toll on Family," *Chicago Sun Times*
   (January 26, 1992): 56.
3. Gary J. Oliver and H. Norman Wright, *When Anger Hits
   Home* (Chicago: Moody Press, 1992), 126.
4. Ibid., 144–45.
5. Ronald Taffel quoted in James A. Levine, "What Fathers
   Want Mothers to Know," *Family Circle* (June 25, 1991): 25.
6. Bill Cosby, *Fatherhood* (New York: Doubleday, 1986), 15.
7. U.S. Bureau of the Census, *Statistical Abstracts of the
   United States: 1950–1988* (Washington, D.C.: U.S.
   Government Printing Office, 1950–1988).
8. W. A. Altemeier, S. O'Connor, P. M. Vietze, H. M. Sandler,
   and K. B. Sherrod, "Antecedents of Child Abuse," *Journal
   of Pediatrics* 100 (1982): 823–29.
9. Michael Lamb, *Fathers and Their Families* (Hillsdale, N.J.:
   Analytic Press, 1989), 16.
10. H. W. Beecher, *The New Dictionary of Thoughts,* ed.
    Tyrone Edwards, (New York: Standard Book Company,
    1957), 462–63.
11. John L. Maes, "Loss and Grief in Fathering," in
    Fathering: Fact or Fable? ed. Edward V. Stein (Nashville:
    Abingdon Press, 1977), 87–107, and Charles A. Corr and
    Joan N. McNeil, *Adolescence and Death* (New York:
    Springer Publishing Co., 1986), 189–91.

12. Jerrold Lee Shapiro, "The Expectant Father," *Psychology Today* (January 1987): 42.

13. Linda Wertheimer quoted in Jamie Diamond, *Lears,* "Personal Glimpses," *Reader's Digest,* May 1992, 88.

Chapter 5

1. Gary Smalley and John Trent, *Love Is a Decision* (Dallas: Word, 1989), 16.

2. Edmund Morgan, *The Puritan Family* (New York: Harper and Row, 1944), 87.

3. Robert Cleaver and John Dod, *A Godly Form of Household Government* (London: 1598), 237–39

4. Martin Greenberg, M.D., *The Birth of a Father* (New York: Continuum, 1985), 18.

5. Carla Cantor, "The Father Factor," *Working Woman,* June 1991, 40–42.

6. Jeanne Block, "Parental Consistency in Child Rearing Orientation and Personality Development." Paper presented at the Annual Convention of the American Psychological Association, Anaheim, Calif., August 26–30, 1983, p. 8.

Chapter 6

1. Glen Elder, *Children of the Great Depression* (Chicago: University of Chicago Press, 1974), 291.

2. John A. McAdoo, "Black Perspective on the Father's Role in Child Development," *Marriage and Family Review* 9:4 (1987): 117–33.

3. Vonnie McLoyd, "Socialization and Development in a Changing Economy," *American Psychologist* 44 (1989): 293–302.

4. Quoted in Dinah Richard, "Has Sex Education Failed Our

Teenagers? A Research Report," *Focus on the Family,* 1990, table 18.

5. Walt Mueller, Telephone interview, October 7, 1992.

6. Ice-T, "The Pickup Artist," *Details,* July 1992, 48.

Chapter 7

1. James A. Levine, "What Fathers Want Mothers to Know," *Family Circle,* June 25, 1991, 23.

2. Ibid.

3. Ibid.

Chapter 8

1. Quoted in Maureen Rank, *Dealing with the Dad of Your Past* (Minneapolis, Minn.: Bethany House, 1990), 18.

2. Suzanne Fields, *Like Father, Like Daughter: How Father Shapes the Woman His Daughter Becomes* (Boston: Little, Brown and Company, 1983), 29.

3. Michael E. Lamb, "The Changing Roles of Fathers," *The Father's Role: Applied Perspectives,* ed. Michael E. Lamb (New York: John Wiley and Sons, 1986), 16–17.

4. Leanne Payne, *Crisis in Masculinity* (Westchester, Ill.: Crossway Books, 1978), 66.

5. Ibid., 68–69.

6. Ibid., 69.

Chapter 9

1. Leanne Payne, *The Healing Presence* (Westchester, Ill.: Crossway Books, 1989), 47.

2. Richard Foster, *Celebration of Discipline* (New York: Harper and Row, 1978), 84.

3. Dallas Willard, *The Spirit of the Disciplines* (San Francisco: Harper Collins, 1988), 157.

4. Ibid.

Chapter 11
1. Gary Smalley, *Love Is a Decision* (Dallas: Word, 1989), 21.

Chapter 12
1. Larry Crabb, "Biblical Masculinity," speech given at Promise Keepers Leadership Training Conference, July 21, 1992.
2. Judson J. Swihart, *How Do You Say "I Love You"?* (Downers Grove, Ill.: InterVarsity Press, 1977), 28–29.

Chapter 13
1. Quoted in James A. Levine, "What Fathers Want Mothers to Know," *Family Circle,* June 25, 1991, 23.
2. James B. Hurley, *Man and Woman in Biblical Perspective* (Grand Rapids, Mich.: Zondervan Publishing House, 1981), 151.

Chapter 14
1. William Whately, *A Bride-Bush or a Direction for Married Persons* (London: STC25299, 1619), 15.
2. Quoted in Karl Stern, *The Flight from Woman* (New York: Farrar, Straus, and Giroux, 1965), 26.

Chapter 15
1. Robert Bly, *Iron John* (Reading, Mass.: Addison-Wesley, 1990), 2–3.